GRADIENTS *of the*
BRITISH MAIN LINE RAILWAYS

GRADIENTS *of the*
BRITISH MAIN LINE RAILWAYS

Ian Allan
PUBLISHING

Gradients of the British Main Line Railways

First published 2016

ISBN 978 0 7110 3844 8

Published by Ian Allan Publishing in collaboration with Tothill Press

an imprint of Ian Allan Publishing Ltd, Addlestone, Surrey KT15 2SF.
Printed in Wales by Gomer Press Ltd.

Visit the Ian Allan Publishing website at www.ianallanpublishing.com

Picture Credits
Every effort has been made to identify and correctly attribute photographic credits. Should any error have occurred this is entirely unintentional.

Front cover: Carlisle Kingmoor-based BR Standard Class 9F No 92019 climbs out of Tebay in June 1957. *Colour-Rail (380057a)*

Rear cover: 'Battle of Britain' No 34060 *25 Squadron* climbs Mortehoe bank with an afternoon train from Ilfracombe to Waterloo. *R. Russell*

Contents

Great Western Railway

Southern Railway

Foreword

The British Rail Main Line Gradient Profiles showing the nationalised BR rail network was originally published by Ian Allan Publishing in 1966 and reprinted many times since then but has been out of print for a number of years.

This new edition goes back to the British railway network on the eve of nationalisation in 1947 so it is effectively the main line network in the last years of the 'Big Four'. It is organised by the separate four companies plus a separate section on joint railways and includes details such as water troughs that were not shown in the previous publication as well as lines that were subsequently closed in the ensuing decade. It also includes for the first time a complete index of all locations shown on the gradient profiles, not only stations but other features such as tunnels, junctions and sidings.

As with earlier editions, a uniform scale of inclination has been adopted throughout, enabling the user to gauge at a glance the relative difficulty of any particular route. The gradient profiles are shown exactly as they were originally reproduced in 1947, with accompanying information from the time given on service slacks, colliery areas where subsidence slacks may reduce speeds, single-line sections, and so on. With the introduction of high-speed trains in the years before World War 2, speed restrictions were introduced that were as high as 70mph, while maximum speeds over certain sections were above 100mph. To represent these the speed restriction indications (see below)* are classified under the headings of 'severe' (30mph or less), 'moderate' (35-55mph), and 'slight' (60mph and over). In the LMSR series of profiles, details are also given of the location of the mileposts, and the zero point from routes are inserted, including the whole line between Shrewsbury and Newport; also for some additional portions of the Southern Railway providing alternative routes between London and Brighton, and between London and Ramsgate; further Welsh coast lines; the line from Inverness to Wick and Thurso, as well as the important branch from Dingwall to Kyle of Lochalsh; the Callander and Oban line; and some sections of the LNER north of Aberdeen.

For ease of reference, all LMSR gradients are numbered with the suffix 'A', the LNER with a 'B', the GWR with a 'C', the SR with a 'D' and joint lines an 'E' and the locations are listed in the index using these profile numbers.

Every gradient is also cross-referenced from one profile to another to facilitate tracing cross-country and connecting routes.

Location of Mileposts

London, Midland & Scottish Railway

Western Division: Down side, from zero at Euston. On the main line from London to Carlisle a second series starts from zero point beyond Warrington; a third series from zero at Preston; and a fourth series from zero at Preston.

Midland Division: Up side, from zero at St Pancras.

Central Division: Down side (relative to Manchester) from zero at Manchester (Victoria).

Northern Division: On Caledonian section, down side from zero at Carlisle. On Glasgow & South Western section down side (relatively to Glasgow) from zero at the original Bridge Street terminus, via Paisley and Dalry. On Highland section, down side (relatively to Inverness) from zero at Inverness.

London & North Eastern Railway

Great Northern Section: Down side, from zero at King's Cross.

Great Eastern Section: Down side, from zero at Liverpool Street.

Great Central Section: Up side, from zero at Manchester (London Road). From Harrow to Quainton Road, down side, from zero at Baker Street (LPTB).

North Eastern Area: Down side (relative to York) from zero at York, except that from Newcastle to Berwick a second series starts from zero at York.

Southern Scottish Area: Down side (relatively to Edinburgh) from zero at Edinburgh (Waverley). This places the posts on the up side relatively to London between Berwick and Edinburgh.

Northern Scottish Area: Down side from zero at Aberdeen.

Great Western Railway

Up side, from zero at Paddington. On the West of England mail line the posts from Westbury to Casle Cary are calculated via Swindon and Trowbridge, and from Taunton onwards via Bristol (Temple Meads). On the North main line a separate series starts from zero at Northolt Junction, and a second separate series from zero at Ashendon Junction; from Aynho Junction (Banbury) onwards the posts are calculated via Oxford. On the South Wales main line the posts from Severn Tunnel Junction onwards are calculated via Gloucester.

Southern Railway

Western Division: Down side from zero at Waterloo.

Eastern Division: Down side, from zero at Charing Cross (SE section) and Victoria (LCD section).

Central Division: Down side, from zero at London Bridge (mileages on Eastern and Central Divisions now reckoned from Charing Cross).

London Midland & Scottish Railway

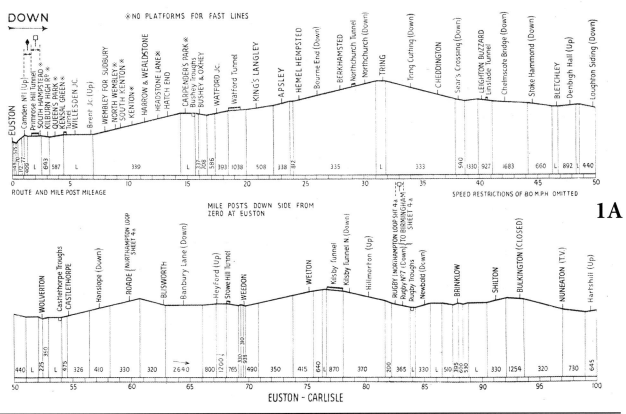

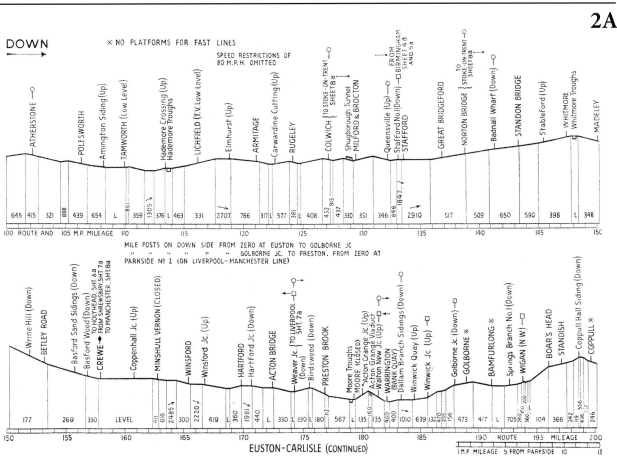

3A DOWN

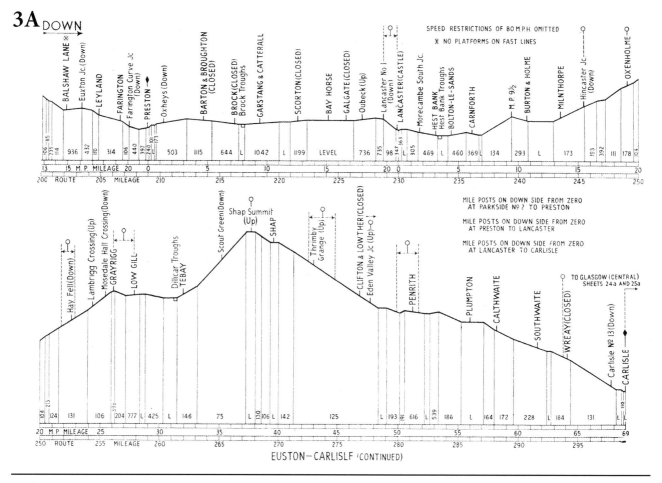

EUSTON–CARLISLE (CONTINUED)

4A

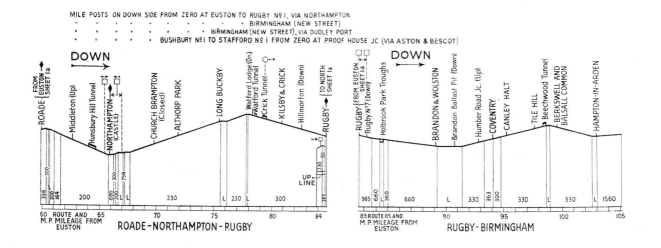

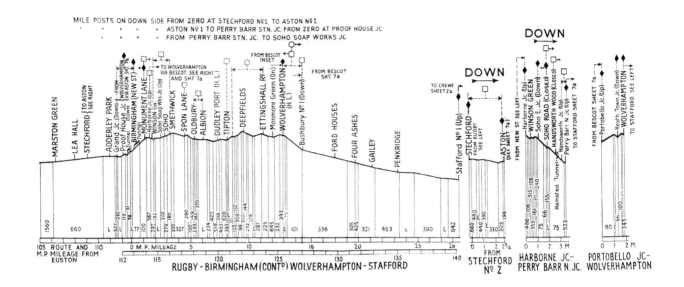

MILE POSTS ON DOWN SIDE FROM ZERO AT STECHFORD Nº1 TO ASTON Nº1
" " " " ASTON Nº 1 TO PERRY BARR STN. JC. FROM ZERO AT PROOF HOUSE JC
" " " " FROM PERRY BARR STN. JC. TO SOHO SOAP WORKS JC.

RUGBY - BIRMINGHAM (CONTᴰ) WOLVERHAMPTON - STAFFORD

FROM STECHFORD Nº 2

HARBORNE JC - PERRY BARR N. JC.

PORTOBELLO JC - WOLVERHAMPTON

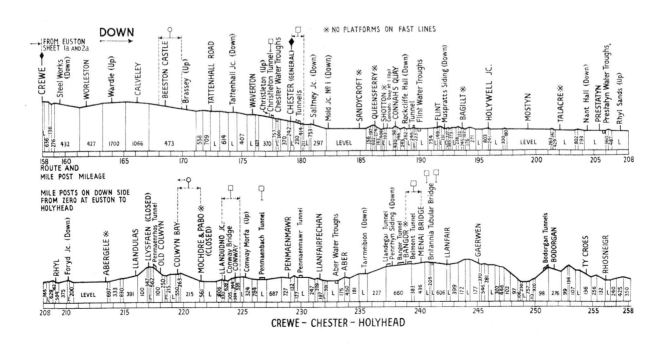

✳ NO PLATFORMS ON FAST LINES

MILE POSTS ON DOWN SIDE FROM ZERO AT EUSTON TO HOLYHEAD

CREWE - CHESTER - HOLYHEAD

7A

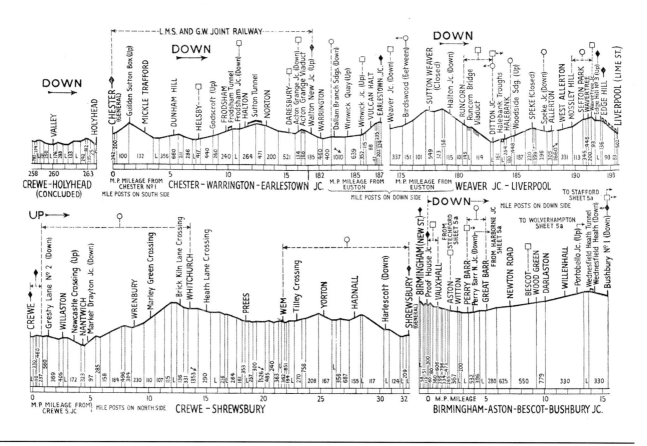

8A

MILE POSTS ON DOWN SIDE EUSTON ZERO TO LONDON ROAD
"   "   "   "   " WILMSLOW ZERO TO SLADE LANE JUNC. VIA STYAL
"   "   "   "   " HEATON NORRIS Nº 2 ZERO TO STALYBRIDGE

MILE POSTS ON DOWN SIDE MACCLESFIELD (H.R.) ZERO TO COLWICH
"   "   "   "   " STONE JUNCTION ZERO TO NORTON BRIDGE
"   "   "   "   " CHEADLE HULME ZERO TO MACCLESFIELD (H.R.)

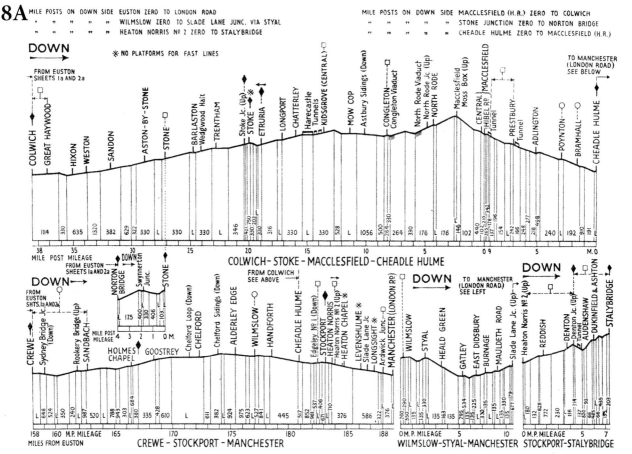

14

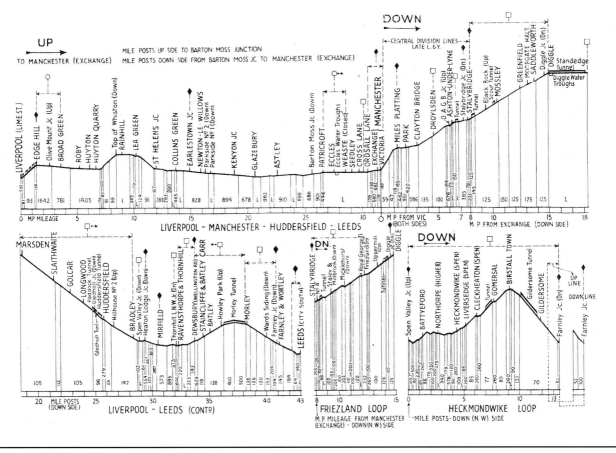

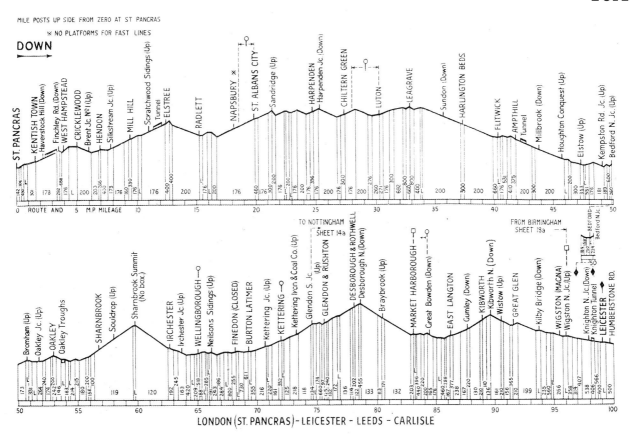

LONDON (ST. PANCRAS)–LEICESTER–LEEDS–CARLISLE

11A

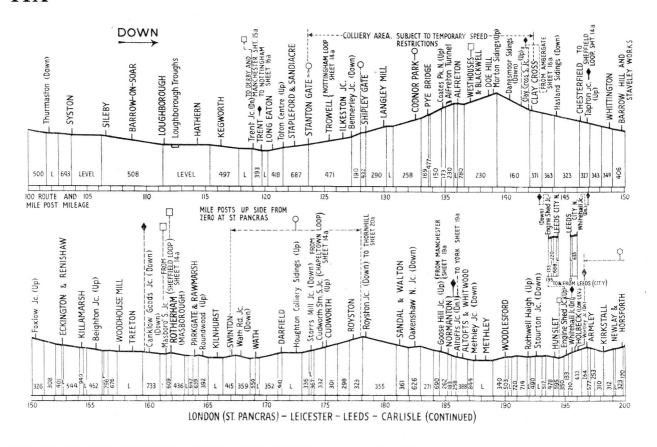

LONDON (ST. PANCRAS) – LEICESTER – LEEDS – CARLISLE (CONTINUED)

12A

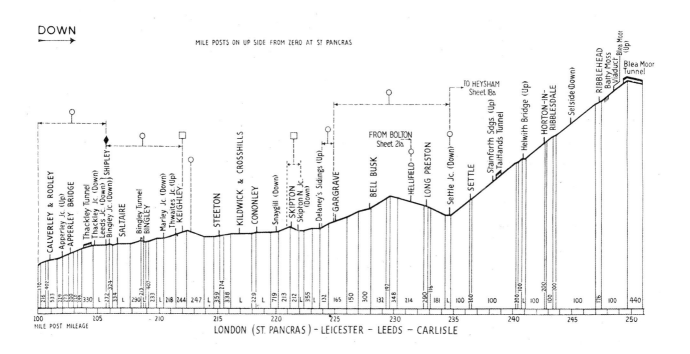

LONDON (ST. PANCRAS) – LEICESTER – LEEDS – CARLISLE

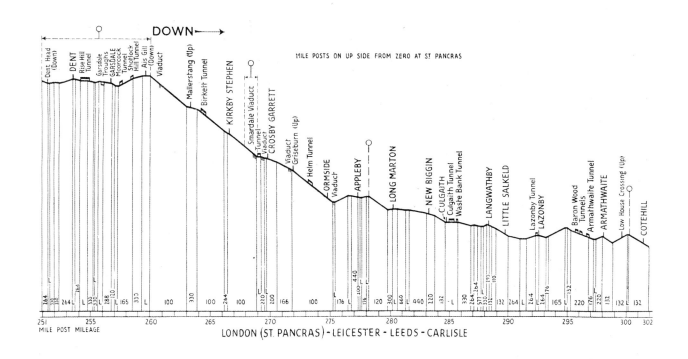

MILE POSTS ON UP SIDE FROM ZERO AT ST PANCRAS

LONDON (ST. PANCRAS) - LEICESTER - LEEDS - CARLISLE

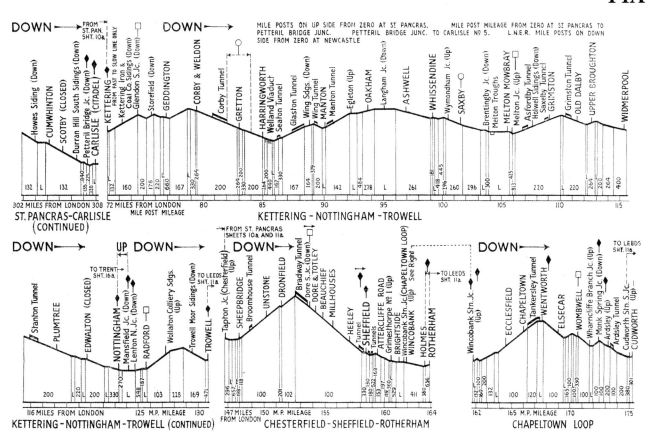

MILE POSTS ON UP SIDE FROM ZERO AT ST PANCRAS.   MILE POST MILEAGE FROM ZERO AT ST PANCRAS TO
PETTERIL BRIDGE JUNC.   PETTERIL BRIDGE JUNC. TO CARLISLE Nº 5.   L.N.E.R. MILE POSTS ON DOWN
SIDE FROM ZERO AT NEWCASTLE

ST. PANCRAS-CARLISLE
(CONTINUED)

KETTERING - NOTTINGHAM - TROWELL

KETTERING - NOTTINGHAM - TROWELL (CONTINUED)

CHESTERFIELD - SHEFFIELD - ROTHERHAM

CHAPELTOWN LOOP

17

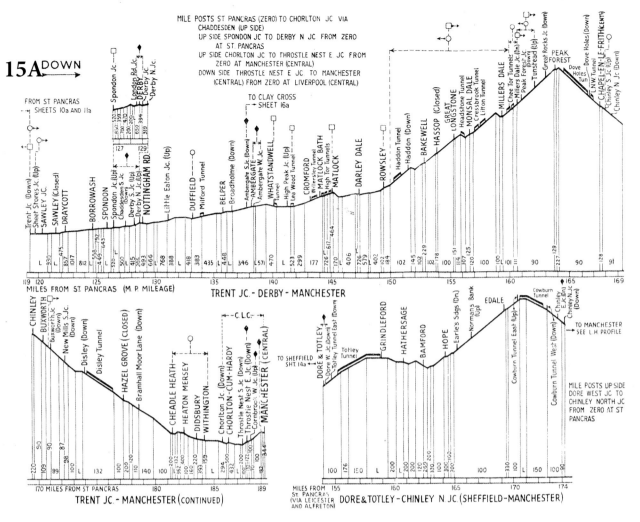

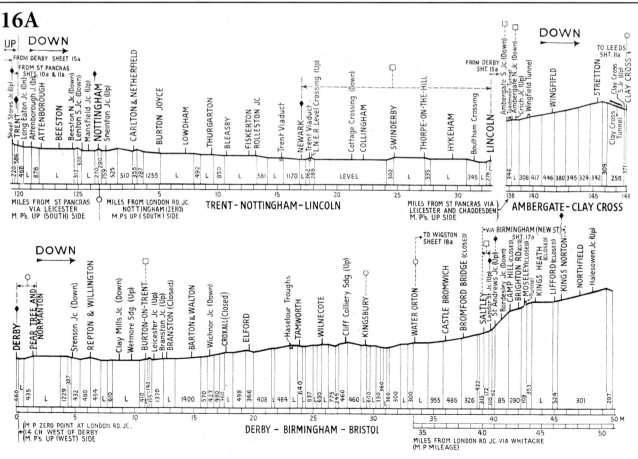

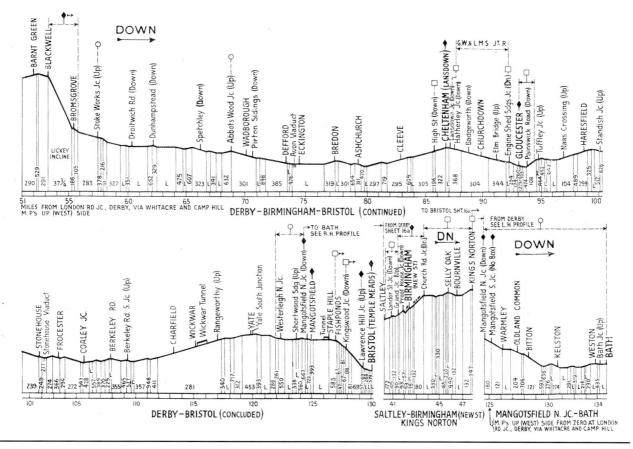

DOWN ►

MILES FROM LONDON RD. JC., DERBY, VIA WHITACRE AND CAMP HILL
M.P's UP (WEST) SIDE

DERBY-BIRMINGHAM-BRISTOL (CONTINUED)

DERBY-BRISTOL (CONCLUDED)

SALTLEY-BIRMINGHAM (NEW ST.) KINGS NORTON

MANGOTSFIELD N. JC.-BATH
M.P's UP (WEST) SIDE FROM ZERO AT LONDON RD. JC., DERBY, VIA WHITACRE AND CAMP HILL

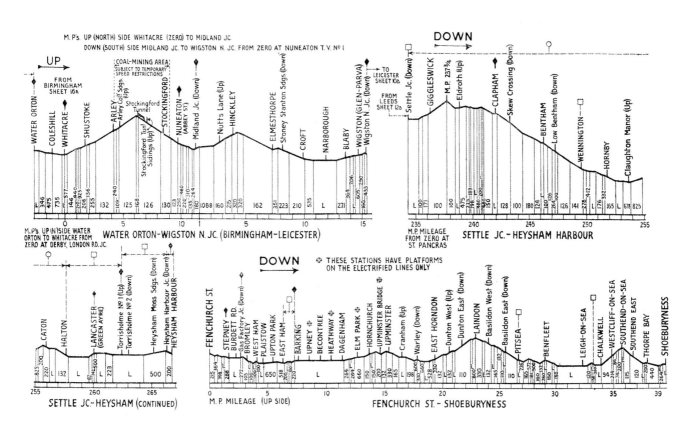

M.P's. UP (NORTH) SIDE WHITACRE (ZERO) TO MIDLAND JC.
DOWN (SOUTH) SIDE MIDLAND JC. TO WIGSTON N. JC. FROM ZERO AT NUNEATON T.V. No 1

UP ►

DOWN ►

M.P's. UP (N) SIDE WATER ORTON TO WHITACRE FROM ZERO AT DERBY, LONDON RD. JC.

WATER ORTON-WIGSTON N. JC. (BIRMINGHAM-LEICESTER)

M.P. MILEAGE FROM ZERO AT ST PANCRAS

SETTLE JC.-HEYSHAM HARBOUR

SETTLE JC.-HEYSHAM (CONTINUED)

DOWN ► ✥ THESE STATIONS HAVE PLATFORMS ON THE ELECTRIFIED LINES ONLY

M.P. MILEAGE (UP SIDE)

FENCHURCH ST.-SHOEBURYNESS

19

19A

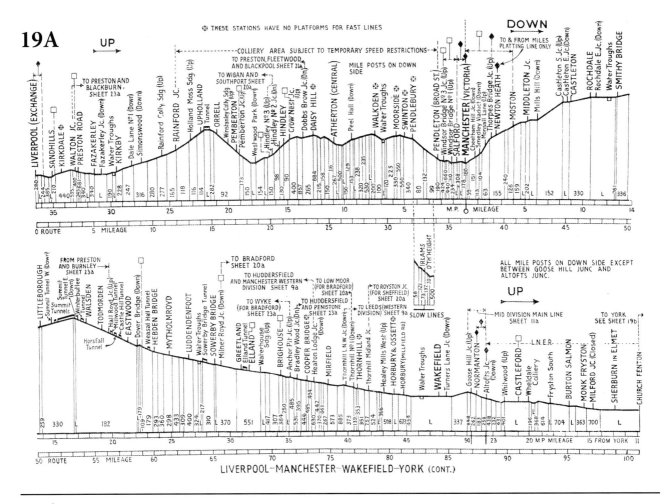

LIVERPOOL—MANCHESTER—WAKEFIELD—YORK (CONT.)

20A

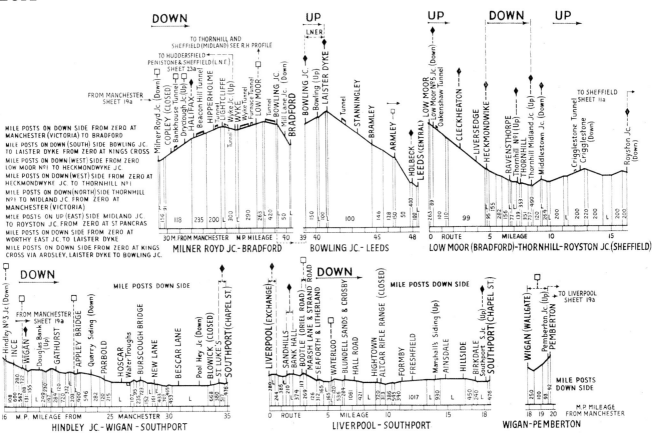

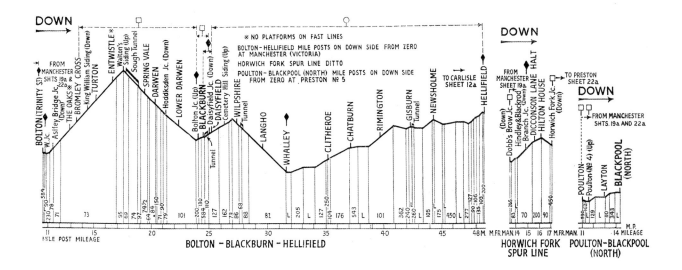

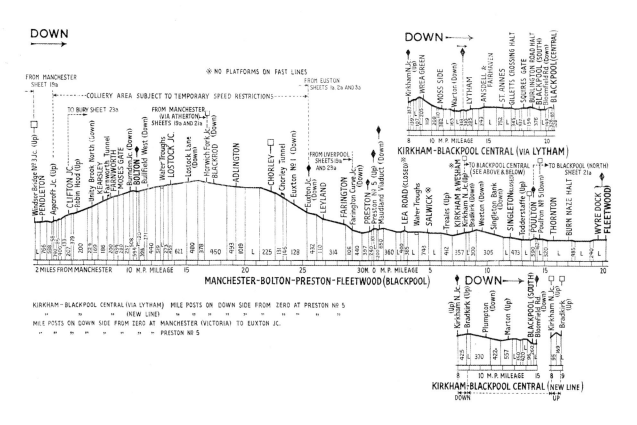

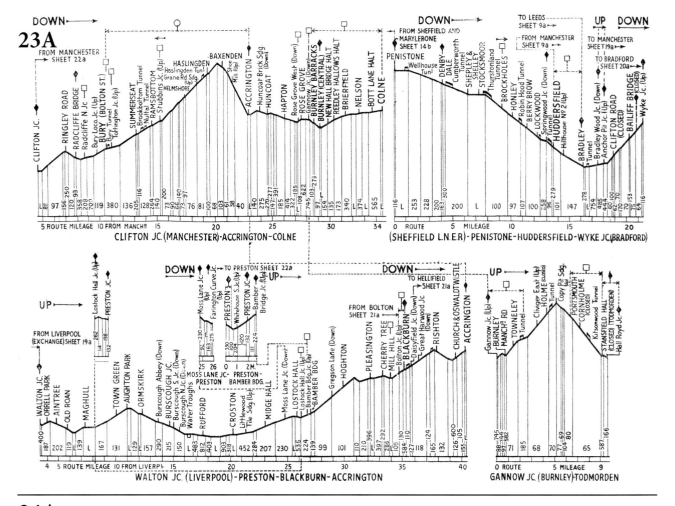

23A

CLIFTON JC. (MANCHESTER)-ACCRINGTON-COLNE

(SHEFFIELD L.N.E.R.)-PENISTONE-HUDDERSFIELD-WYKE JC.(BRADFORD)

WALTON JC. (LIVERPOOL)-PRESTON-BLACKBURN-ACCRINGTON

GANNOW JC. (BURNLEY)-TODMORDEN

24A

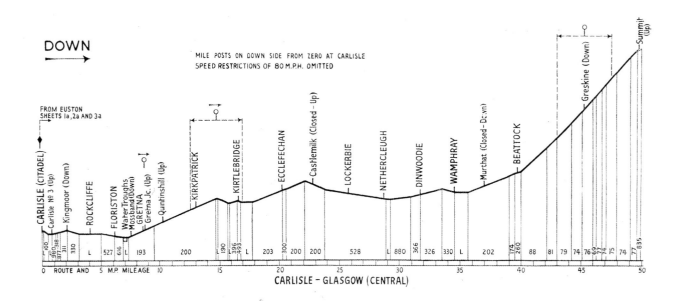

CARLISLE - GLASGOW (CENTRAL)

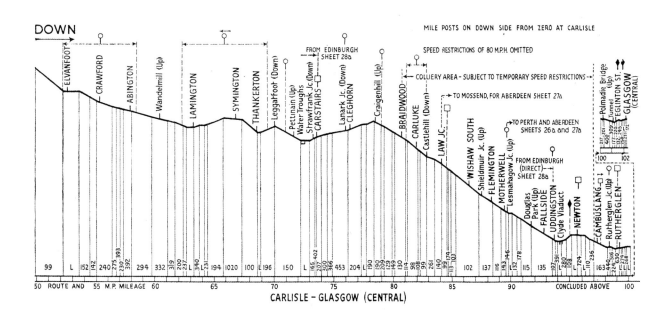

DOWN →

MILE POSTS ON DOWN SIDE FROM ZERO AT CARLISLE

SPEED RESTRICTIONS OF 80 M.P.H. OMITTED

CARLISLE – GLASGOW (CENTRAL)

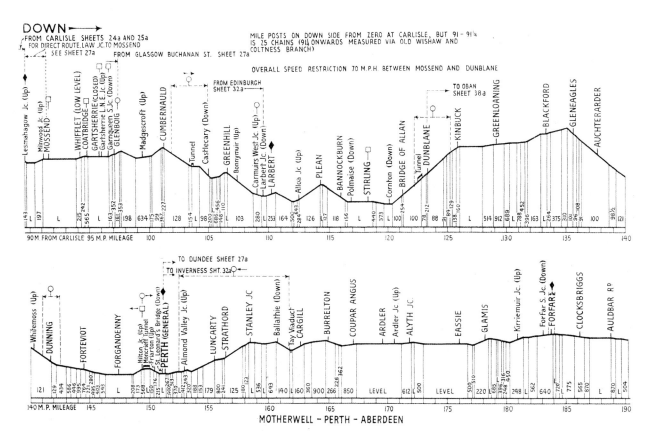

DOWN →

MILE POSTS ON DOWN SIDE FROM ZERO AT CARLISLE, BUT 91 - 91¼
IS 25 CHAINS (91¼ ONWARDS MEASURED VIA OLD WISHAW AND
COLTNESS BRANCH)

OVERALL SPEED RESTRICTION 70 M.P.H. BETWEEN MOSSEND AND DUNBLANE

MOTHERWELL – PERTH – ABERDEEN

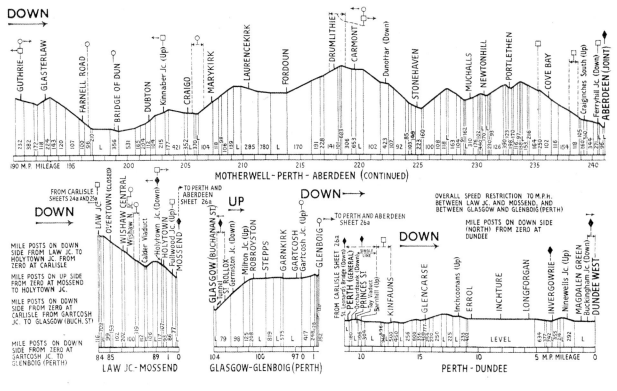

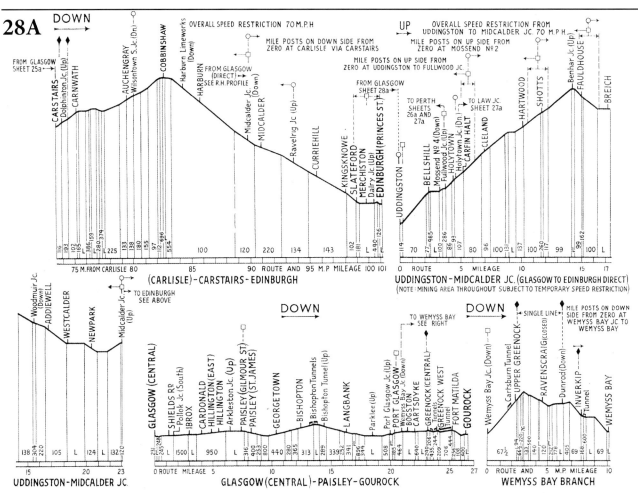

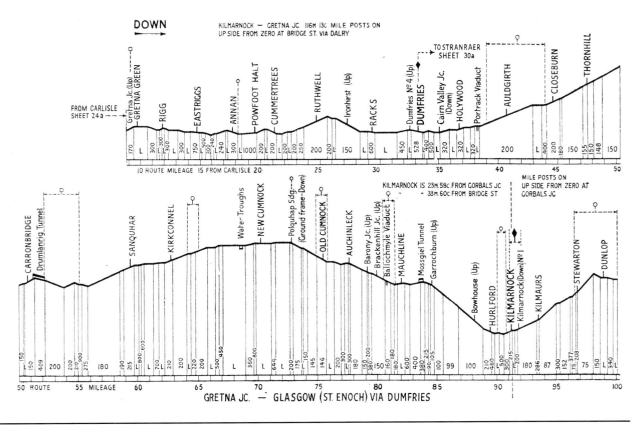

DOWN

KILMARNOCK — GRETNA JC. 116M 13c MILE POSTS ON
UP SIDE FROM ZERO AT BRIDGE ST. VIA DALRY

GRETNA JC. — GLASGOW (ST. ENOCH) VIA DUMFRIES

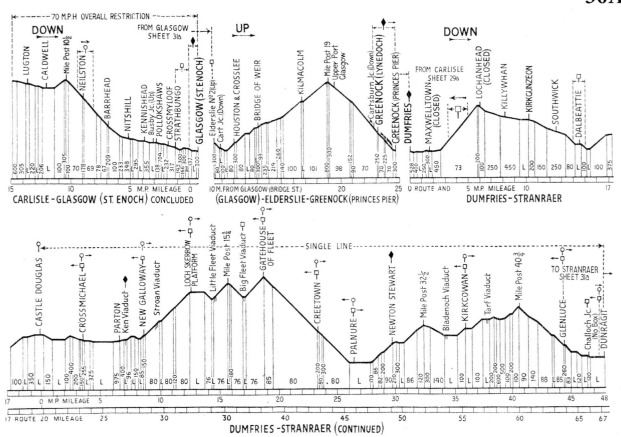

CARLISLE-GLASGOW (ST. ENOCH) CONCLUDED

(GLASGOW)-ELDERSLIE-GREENOCK (PRINCES PIER)

DUMFRIES-STRANRAER

DUMFRIES-STRANRAER (CONTINUED)

31A

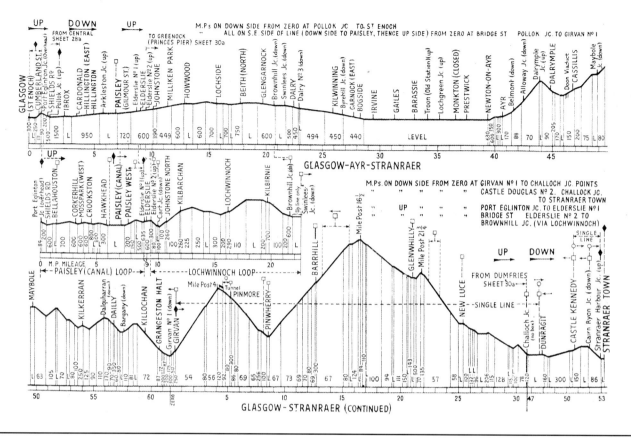

GLASGOW-AYR-STRANRAER

GLASGOW-STRANRAER (CONTINUED)

32A

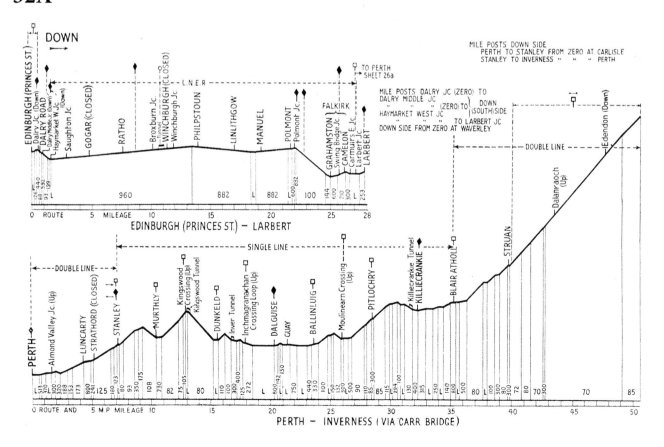

EDINBURGH (PRINCES ST.) – LARBERT

PERTH – INVERNESS (VIA CARR BRIDGE)

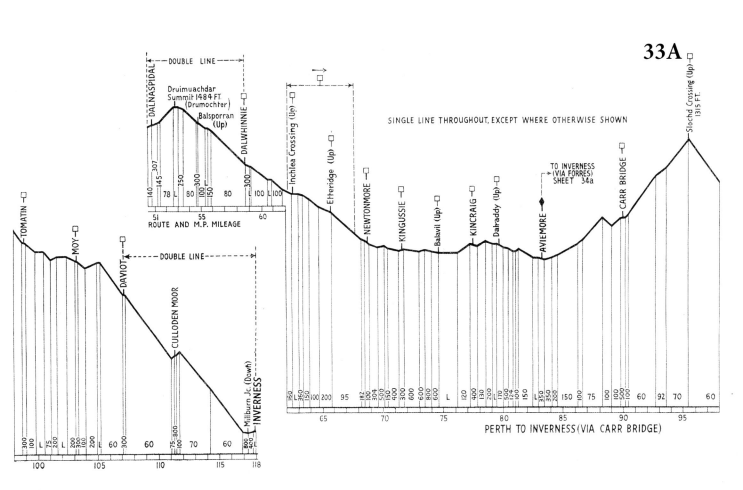

SINGLE LINE THROUGHOUT, EXCEPT WHERE OTHERWISE SHOWN

PERTH TO INVERNESS (VIA CARR BRIDGE)

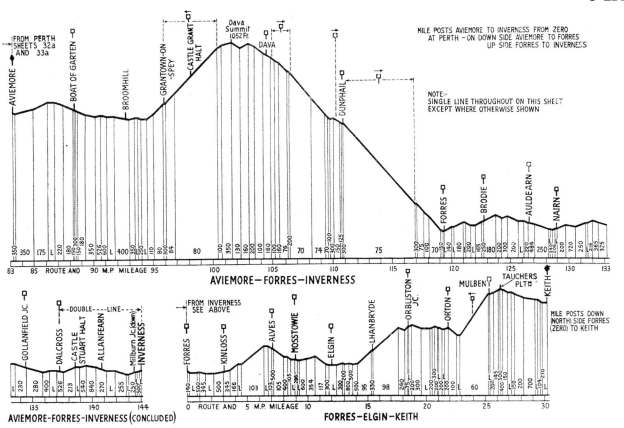

MILE POSTS AVIEMORE TO INVERNESS FROM ZERO
AT PERTH - ON DOWN SIDE AVIEMORE TO FORRES
UP SIDE FORRES TO INVERNESS

NOTE:-
SINGLE LINE THROUGHOUT ON THIS SHEET
EXCEPT WHERE OTHERWISE SHOWN

AVIEMORE—FORRES—INVERNESS

MILE POSTS DOWN
(NORTH) SIDE FORRES
(ZERO) TO KEITH

AVIEMORE-FORRES-INVERNESS (CONCLUDED)

FORRES-ELGIN-KEITH

35A

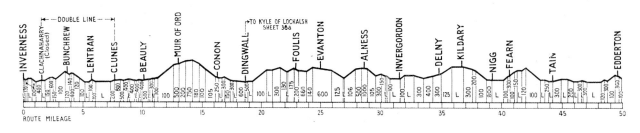

INVERNESS TO WICK: SINGLE LINE THROUGHOUT,
EXCEPT AS INDICATED

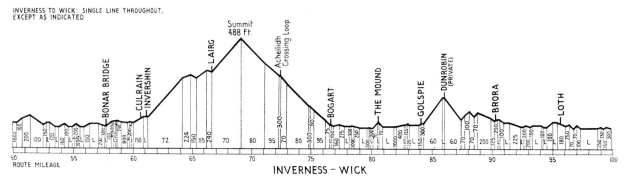

INVERNESS — WICK

Speed restrictions are too numerous to warrant their inclusion

36A

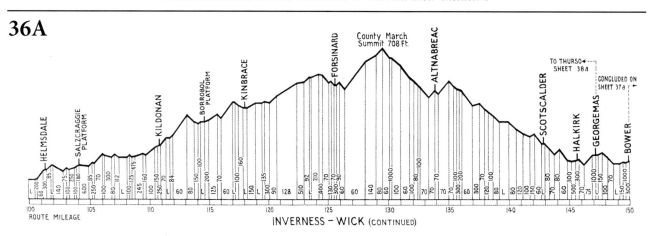

INVERNESS — WICK (CONTINUED)

DINGWALL TO KYLE OF LOCHALSH
SINGLE LINE THROUGHOUT

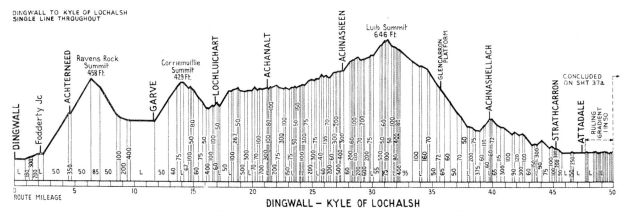

DINGWALL — KYLE OF LOCHALSH

Speed restrictions are too numerous to warrant their inclusion

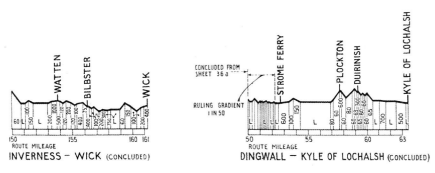

Speed restrictions are too numerous to warrant their inclusion.

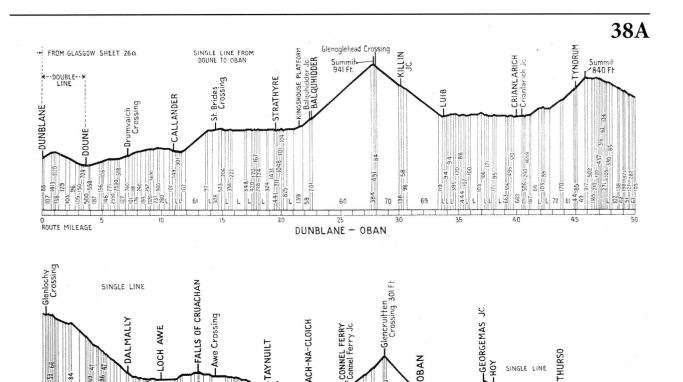

Speed restrictions are too numerous to warrant their inclusion

London & North Eastern Railway

1B

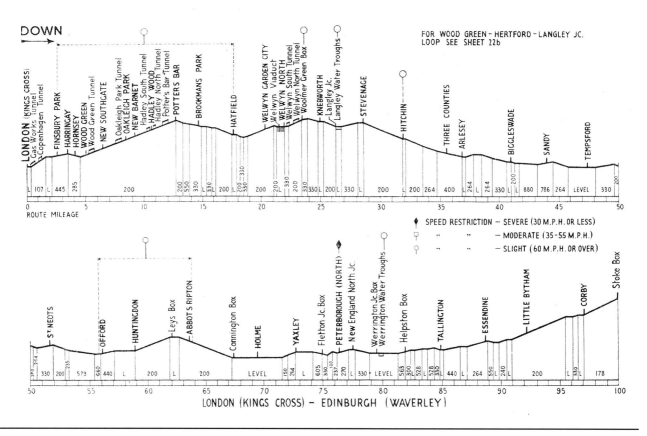

LONDON (KINGS CROSS) – EDINBURGH (WAVERLEY)

2B

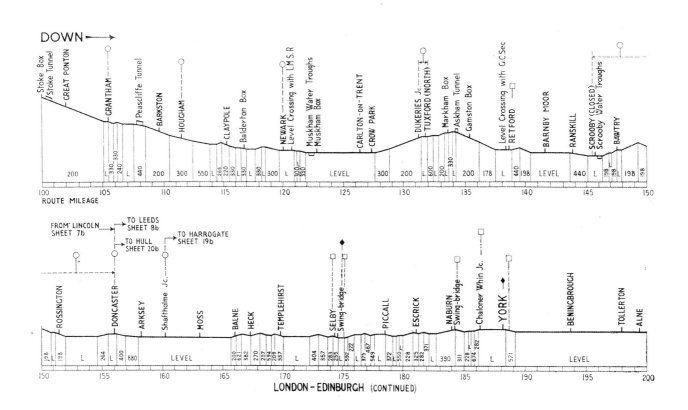

LONDON – EDINBURGH (CONTINUED)

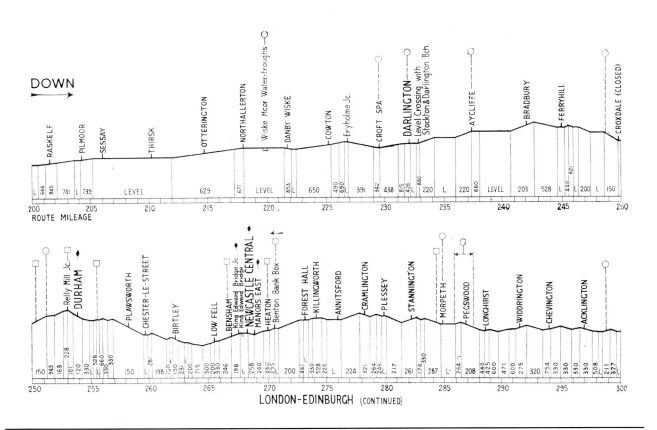

DOWN →

RASKELF · PILMOOR · SESSAY · THIRSK · OTTERINGTON · NORTHALLERTON · Wiske Moor Water-troughs · DANBY WISKE · COWTON · Eryholme Jc. · CROFT SPA · DARLINGTON · Level Crossing with Stockton & Darlington Bch. · AYCLIFFE · BRADBURY · FERRYHILL · CROXDALE (CLOSED)

L 666 845 | 741 L 739 | LEVEL | 629 | 671 LEVEL | 853 | 650 | 490 690 | 391 | 342 438 | 815 426 860 | 220 | L | 220 660 | LEVEL | 203 | 528 | 440 L 200 | L 150

200 · 205 · 210 · 215 · 220 · 225 · 230 · 235 · 240 · 245 · 250
ROUTE MILEAGE

Relly Mill Jc. · DURHAM · PLAWSWORTH · CHESTER-LE-STREET · BIRTLEY · LOW FELL · BENSHAM · King Edward Bridge Jc. · King Edward Bridge · NEWCASTLE CENTRAL · MANORS EAST · HEATON · Benton Bank Box · FOREST HALL · KILLINGWORTH · ANNITSFORD · CRAMLINGTON · PLESSEY · STANNINGTON · MORPETH · PEGSWOOD · LONGHIRST · WIDDRINGTON · CHEVINGTON · ACKLINGTON

150 943 163 | 228 101 120 | 330 650 660 330 | 150 | 281 | 198 150 231 | 500 200 330 | 246 198 | 258 240 969 275 | 200 | 461 L | 330 528 220 | L | 224 | 321 264 246 | 217 | 261 | 174 330 | 287 | L 264 | 208 | 440 425 600 | 471 | 600 275 | 320 | 754 330 | 330 | 330 | 508 211 377 L

250 · 255 · 260 · 265 · 270 · 275 · 280 · 285 · 290 · 295 · 300

LONDON-EDINBURGH (CONTINUED)

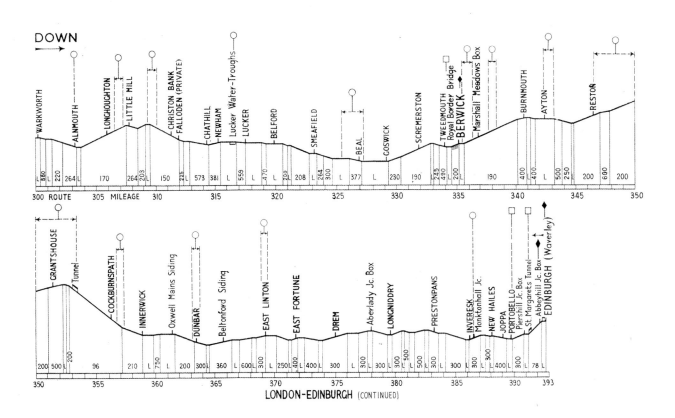

DOWN →

WARKWORTH · ALNMOUTH · LONGHOUGHTON · LITTLE MILL · CHRISTON BANK · FALLODEN (PRIVATE) · CHATHILL · NEWHAM · Lucker Water-Troughs · LUCKER · BELFORD · SMEAFIELD · BEAL · GOSWICK · SCREMERSTON · TWEEDMOUTH · Royal Border Bridge · BERWICK · Marshall Meadows Box · BURNMOUTH · AYTON · RESTON

L 880 L 220 L 264 L | 170 | 264 203 L | 150 | 225 L 573 381 L | 559 | 470 L 200 | 208 | 264 300 | L 377 L | 230 | 190 | 245 490 L 200 L | 190 | 400 | 400 L | 500 250 L | 200 | 600 | 200

300 ROUTE · 305 MILEAGE · 310 · 315 · 320 · 325 · 330 · 335 · 340 · 345 · 350

GRANTSHOUSE · Tunnel · COCKBURNSPATH · INNERWICK · Oxwell Mains Siding · DUNBAR · Beltonford Siding · EAST LINTON · EAST FORTUNE · DREM · Aberlady Jc. Box · LONGNIDDRY · PRESTONPANS · INVERESK · Monktonhall Jc. · NEW HAILES · JOPPA · PORTOBELLO · Piershill Jc. Box · St. Margarets Tunnel · Abbeyhill Jc. Box · EDINBURGH (Waverley)

200 500 L | 200 | 96 | 210 L 750 L | 200 300 L | 360 | L 600 L | 300 | L 250 L | 400 L 400 L | 300 | L 300 | L 300 | L 500 | 300 | L 300 | 300 | L 400 L | 300 | L 78 L

350 · 355 · 360 · 365 · 370 · 375 · 380 · 385 · 390 · 393

LONDON-EDINBURGH (CONTINUED)

5B

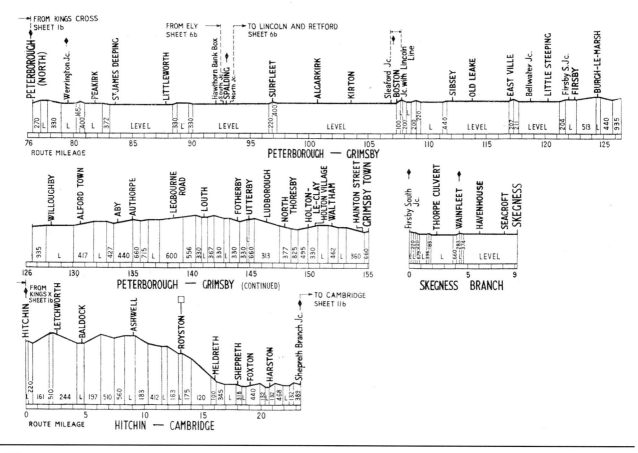

6B

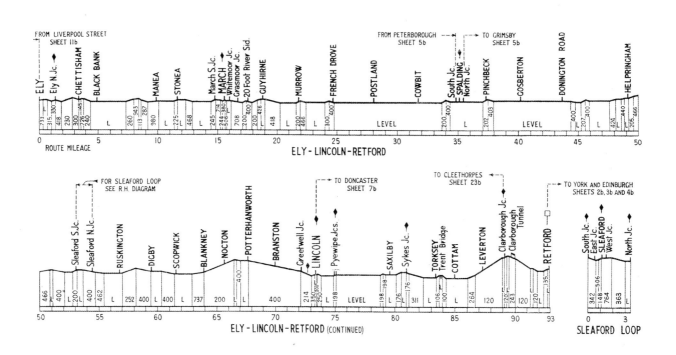

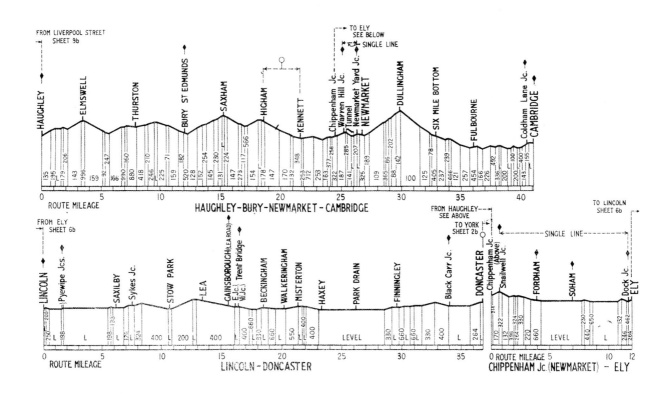

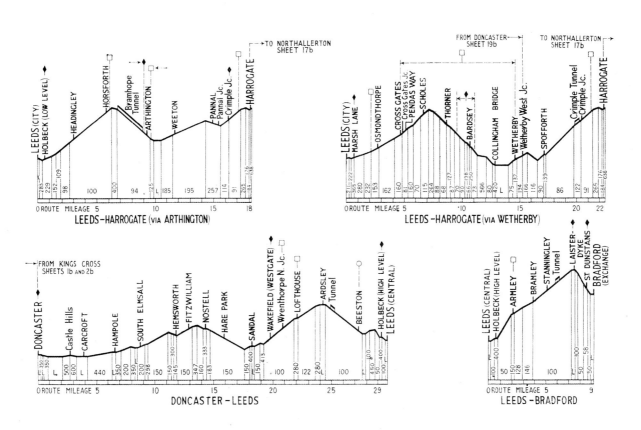

9B

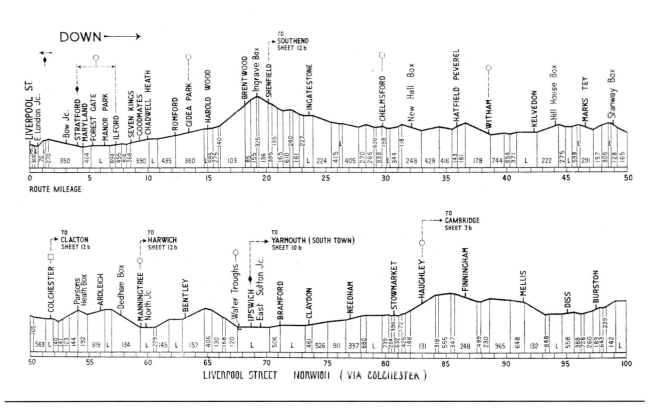

DOWN⟶

ROUTE MILEAGE

LIVERPOOL STREET   NORWICH (VIA COLCHESTER)

10B

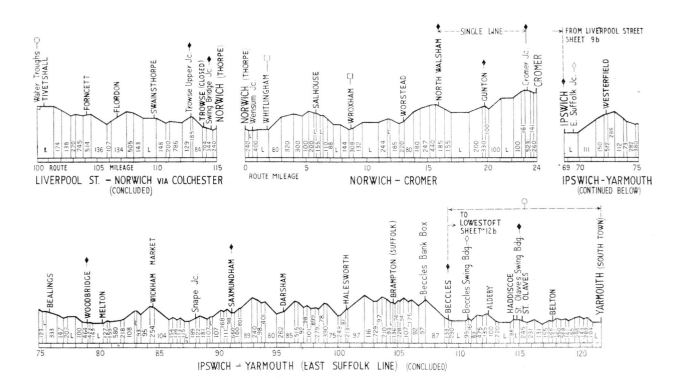

LIVERPOOL ST. – NORWICH via COLCHESTER
(CONCLUDED)

ROUTE MILEAGE

NORWICH – CROMER

IPSWICH – YARMOUTH
(CONTINUED BELOW)

IPSWICH – YARMOUTH (EAST SUFFOLK LINE) (CONCLUDED)

11B

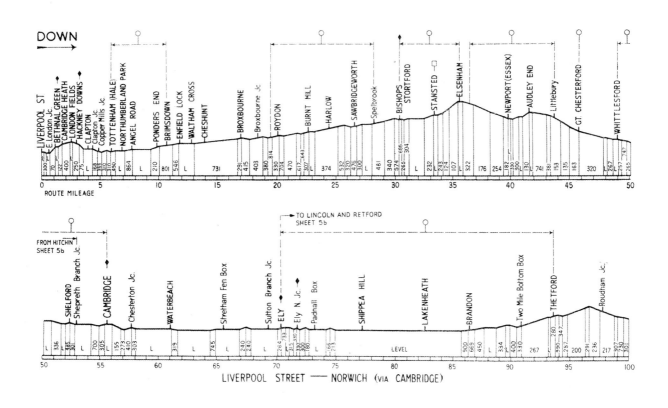

DOWN →

ROUTE MILEAGE

LIVERPOOL STREET — NORWICH (via CAMBRIDGE)

12B

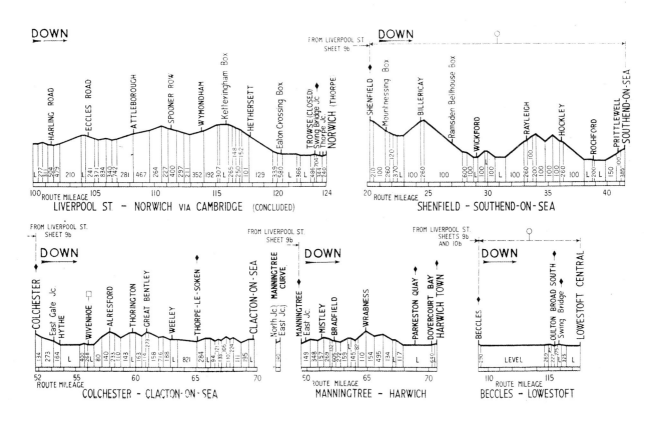

DOWN →

LIVERPOOL ST. – NORWICH via CAMBRIDGE (CONCLUDED)

DOWN →

SHENFIELD – SOUTHEND-ON-SEA

FROM LIVERPOOL ST.
SHEET 9b

DOWN →

COLCHESTER – CLACTON-ON-SEA

FROM LIVERPOOL ST.
SHEET 9b

DOWN →

MANNINGTREE – HARWICH

FROM LIVERPOOL ST.
SHEETS 9b AND 10b

DOWN →

BECCLES – LOWESTOFT

13B

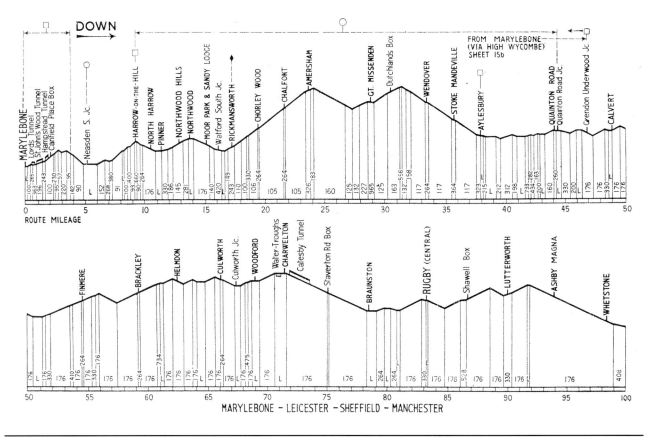

ROUTE MILEAGE

MARYLEBONE – LEICESTER – SHEFFIELD – MANCHESTER

14B

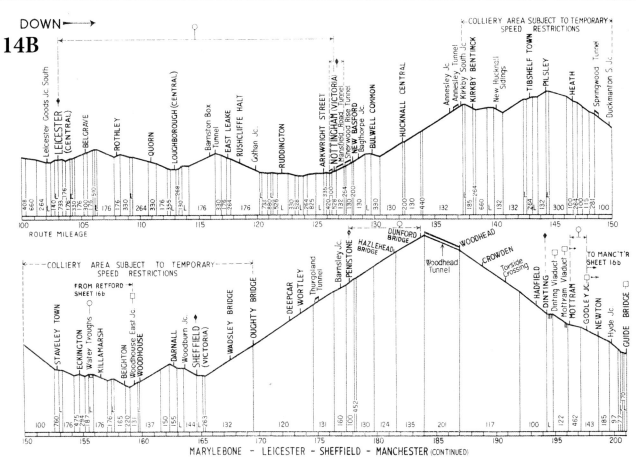

ROUTE MILEAGE

MARYLEBONE – LEICESTER – SHEFFIELD – MANCHESTER (CONTINUED)

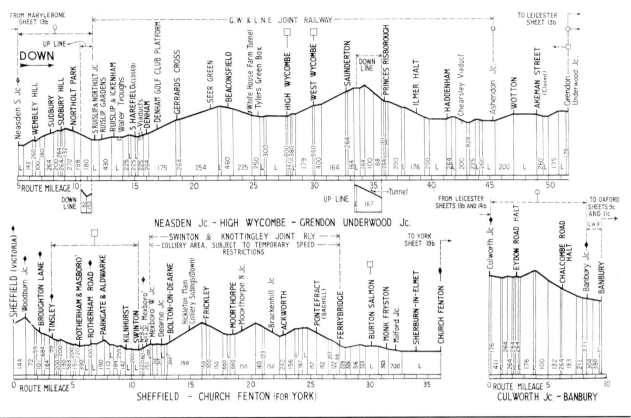

NEASDEN Jc. - HIGH WYCOMBE - GRENDON UNDERWOOD Jc.

SHEFFIELD - CHURCH FENTON (FOR YORK)

CULWORTH Jc. - BANBURY

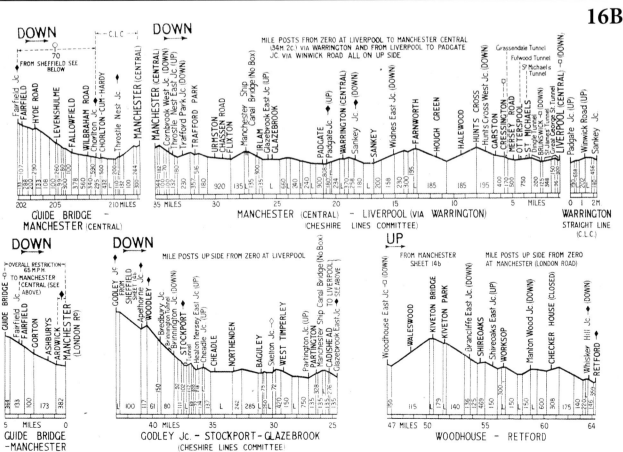

GUIDE BRIDGE - MANCHESTER (CENTRAL)

MANCHESTER (CENTRAL) - LIVERPOOL (VIA WARRINGTON)
(CHESHIRE LINES COMMITTEE)

WARRINGTON
STRAIGHT LINE
(C.L.C.)

GUIDE BRIDGE - MANCHESTER (LONDON ROAD)

GODLEY Jc. - STOCKPORT - GLAZEBROOK
(CHESHIRE LINES COMMITTEE)

WOODHOUSE - RETFORD

37

17B

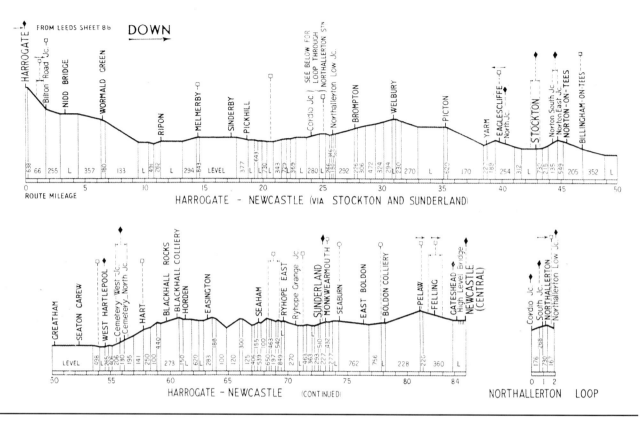

HARROGATE — NEWCASTLE (VIA STOCKTON AND SUNDERLAND)

HARROGATE — NEWCASTLE (CONTINUED)

NORTHALLERTON LOOP

18B

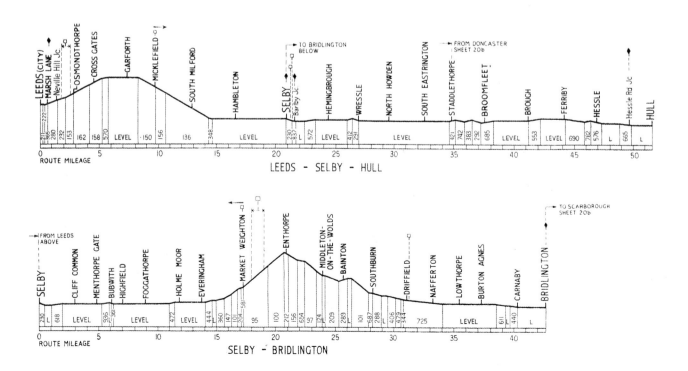

LEEDS — SELBY — HULL

SELBY — BRIDLINGTON

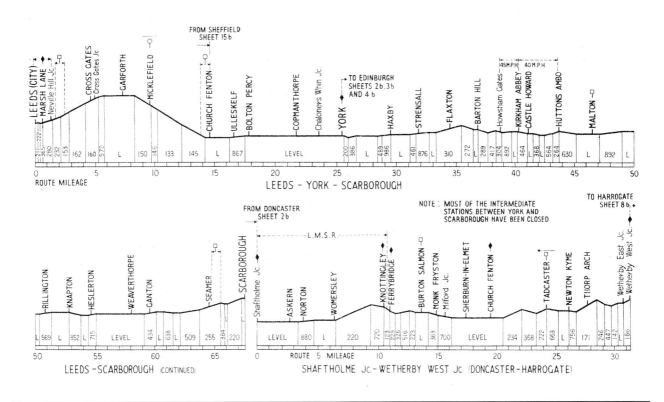

LEEDS - YORK - SCARBOROUGH

LEEDS - SCARBOROUGH (CONTINUED)

SHAFTHOLME Jc.- WETHERBY WEST Jc. (DONCASTER-HARROGATE)

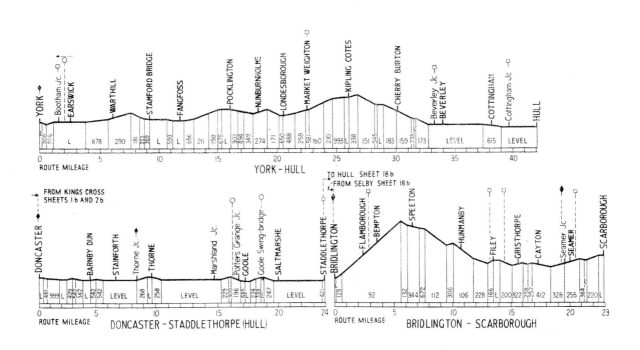

YORK - HULL

DONCASTER - STADDLETHORPE (HULL)

BRIDLINGTON - SCARBOROUGH

21B

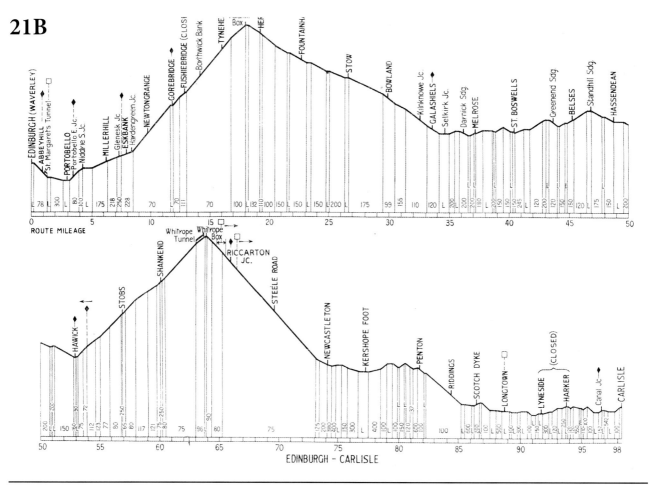

EDINBURGH - CARLISLE

22B

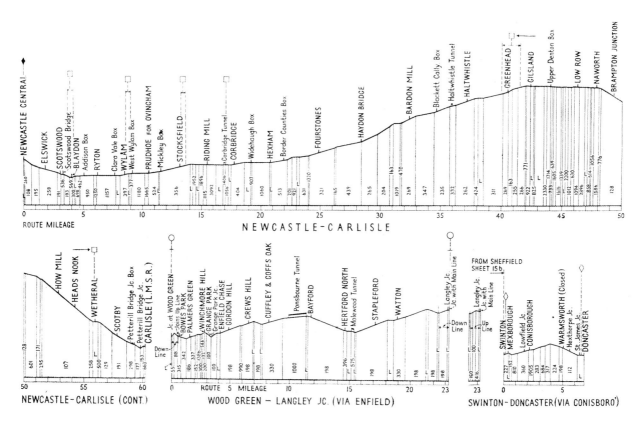

NEWCASTLE-CARLISLE

NEWCASTLE-CARLISLE (CONT.)   WOOD GREEN — LANGLEY JC. (VIA ENFIELD)   SWINTON-DONCASTER (VIA CONISBORO')

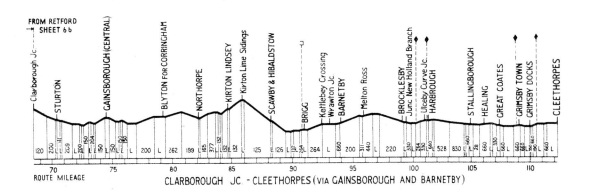

CLARBOROUGH JC. - CLEETHORPES (VIA GAINSBOROUGH AND BARNETBY)

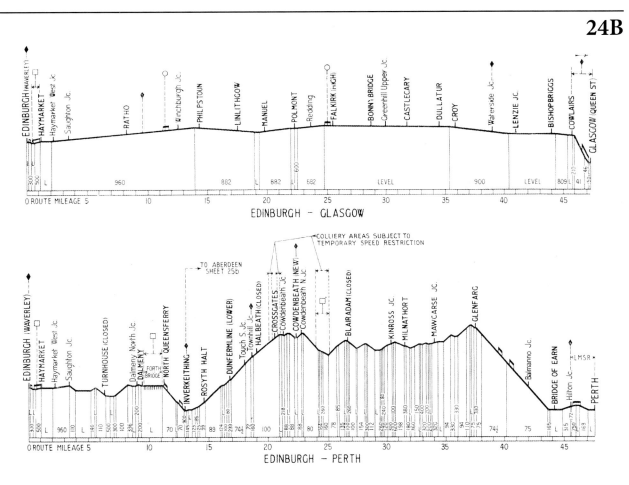

EDINBURGH - GLASGOW

EDINBURGH - PERTH

25B

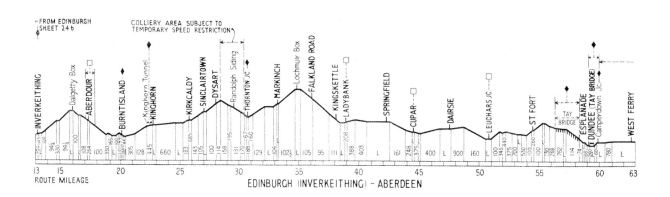

FROM EDINBURGH
SHEET 24 b

COLLIERY AREA SUBJECT TO
TEMPORARY SPEED RESTRICTION

EDINBURGH (INVERKEITHING) - ABERDEEN

ROUTE MILEAGE

26B

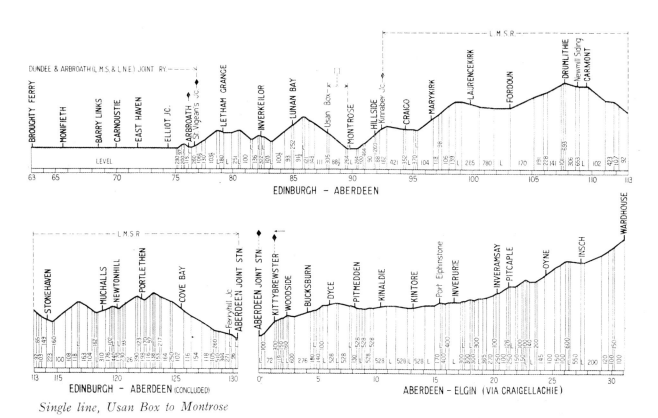

DUNDEE & ARBROATH (L.M.S.&L.N.E.) JOINT RY.

L.M.S.R.

EDINBURGH - ABERDEEN

L.M.S.R.

EDINBURGH - ABERDEEN (CONCLUDED)

ABERDEEN - ELGIN (VIA CRAIGELLACHIE)

Single line, Usan Box to Montrose

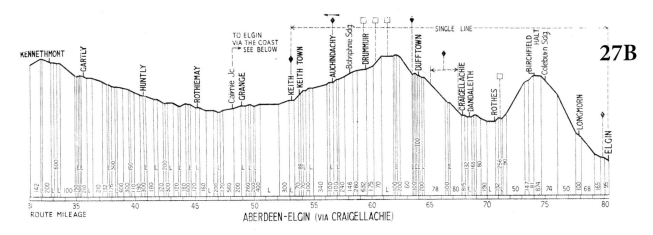

27B

ABERDEEN-ELGIN (VIA CRAIGELLACHIE)

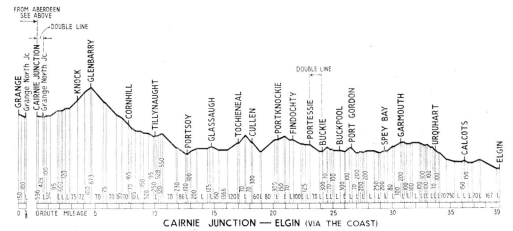

CAIRNIE JUNCTION — ELGIN (VIA THE COAST)

Speed restrictions are too numerous to warrant their inclusion
Single line Cairnie Junction to Elgin, via *the Coast, except as noted*

28B

Single line, Park to Ballater

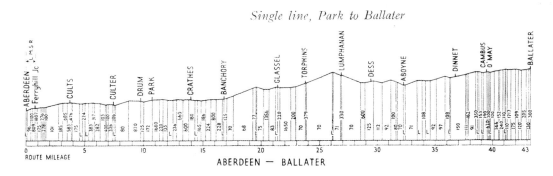

ABERDEEN — BALLATER

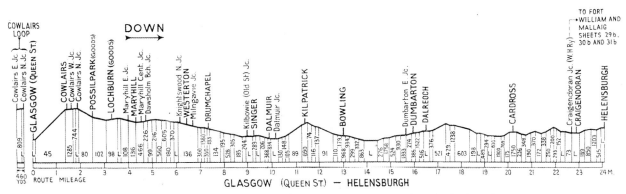

GLASGOW (QUEEN ST.) — HELENSBURGH

Speed restrictions are too numerous to warrant their inclusion

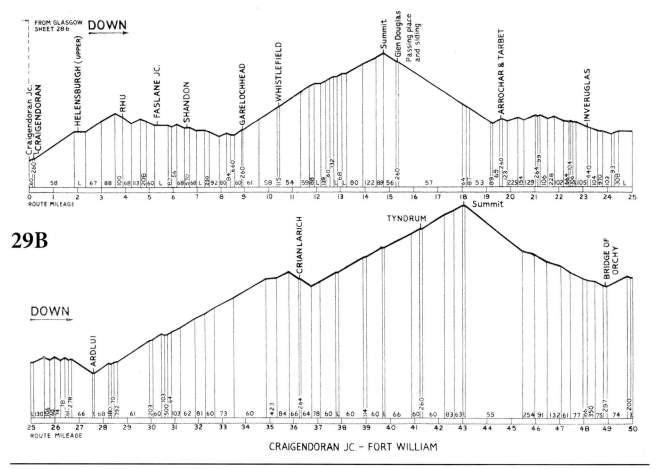

29B

CRAIGENDORAN JC. – FORT WILLIAM

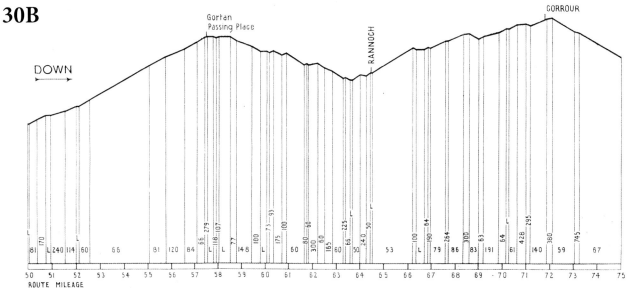

30B

CRAIGENDORAN JC. — FORT WILLIAM

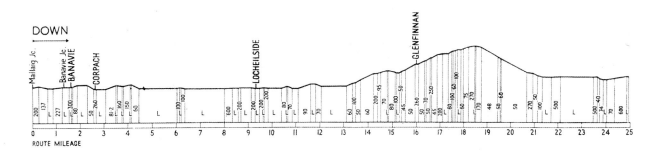

DOWN →

MALLAIG JC. — MALLAIG

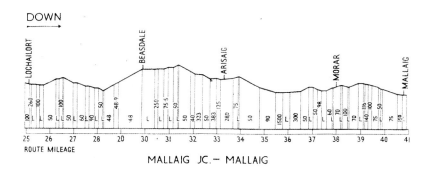

DOWN →

ALL SINGLE LINE EXCEPT BETWEEN ABERDEEN AND DYCE

ABERDEEN — MAUD — PETERHEAD

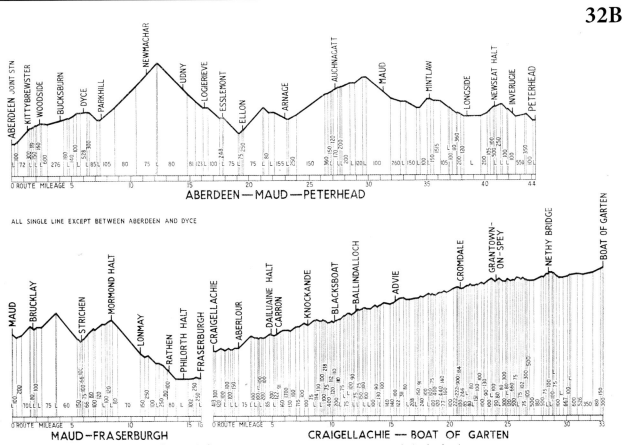

MAUD — FRASERBURGH

CRAIGELLACHIE — BOAT OF GARTEN

Speed restrictions are too numerous to warrant their inclusion

Great Western Railway

1C

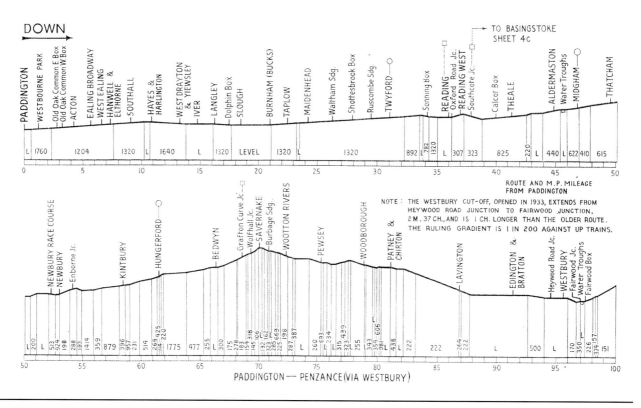

PADDINGTON — PENZANCE (VIA WESTBURY)

ROUTE AND M.P. MILEAGE FROM PADDINGTON

NOTE : THE WESTBURY CUT-OFF, OPENED IN 1933, EXTENDS FROM HEYWOOD ROAD JUNCTION TO FAIRWOOD JUNCTION, 2 M . 37 CH., AND IS 1 CH. LONGER THAN THE OLDER ROUTE. THE RULING GRADIENT IS 1 IN 200 AGAINST UP TRAINS.

2C

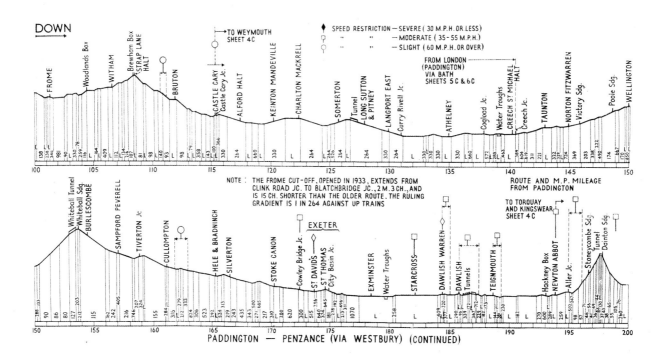

NOTE : THE FROME CUT-OFF, OPENED IN 1933, EXTENDS FROM CLINK ROAD JC. TO BLATCHBRIDGE JC., 2 M. 3 CH., AND IS 15 CH. SHORTER THAN THE OLDER ROUTE. THE RULING GRADIENT IS 1 IN 264 AGAINST UP TRAINS

ROUTE AND M.P. MILEAGE FROM PADDINGTON

PADDINGTON — PENZANCE (VIA WESTBURY) (CONTINUED)

DOWN

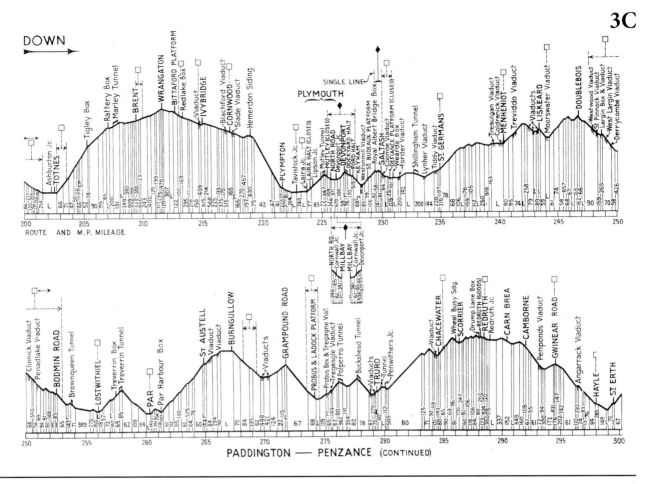

ROUTE AND M.P. MILEAGE

PADDINGTON — PENZANCE (CONTINUED)

DOWN

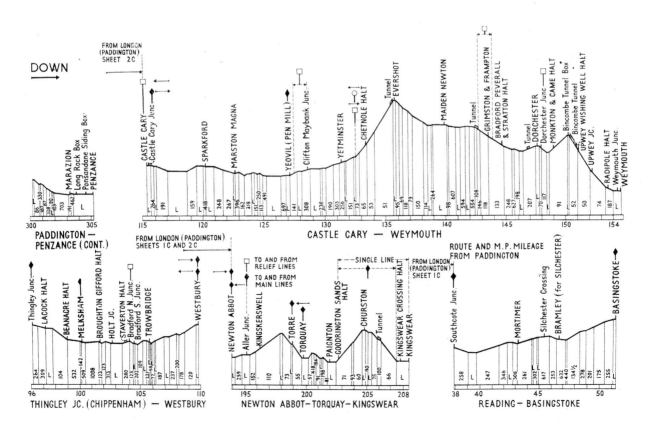

PADDINGTON — PENZANCE (CONT.)

CASTLE CARY — WEYMOUTH

THINGLEY JC. (CHIPPENHAM) — WESTBURY

NEWTON ABBOT—TORQUAY—KINGSWEAR

READING — BASINGSTOKE

5C

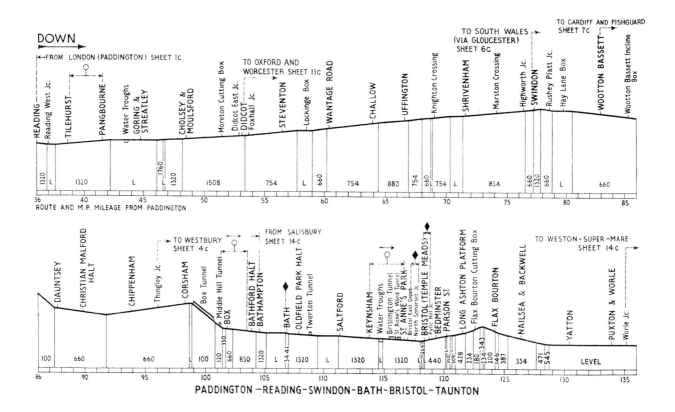

PADDINGTON —READING—SWINDON—BATH—BRISTOL—TAUNTON

6C

The main lines to the West, via Bristol and Westbury respectively, meet at Cogload Junction, but join at Creech Junction. The down Bristol line is carried over the Westbury lines, and has slightly altered gradients between Durston and Creech Junction

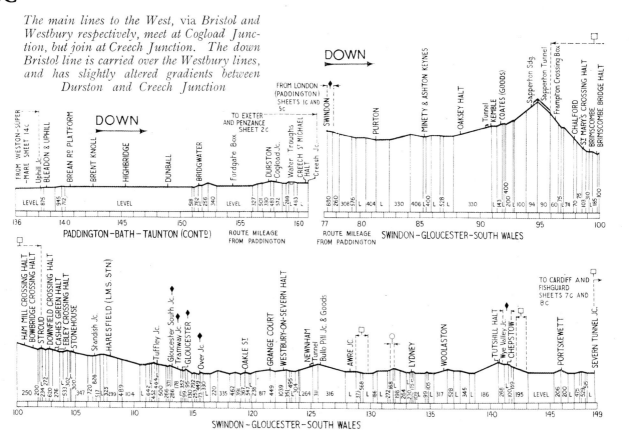

PADDINGTON—BATH—TAUNTON (CONTD.)

SWINDON—GLOUCESTER—SOUTH WALES

SWINDON—GLOUCESTER—SOUTH WALES

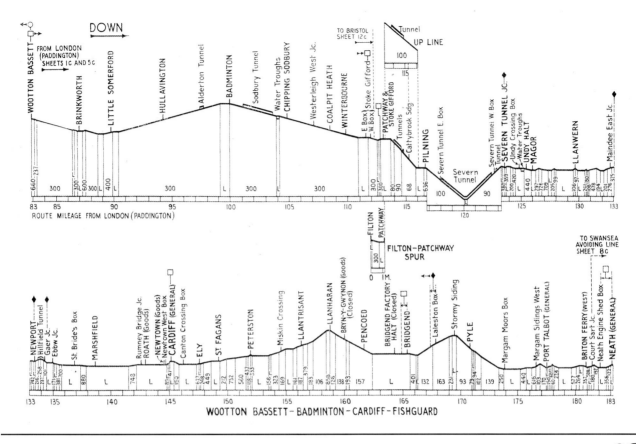

WOOTTON BASSETT – BADMINTON – CARDIFF – FISHGUARD

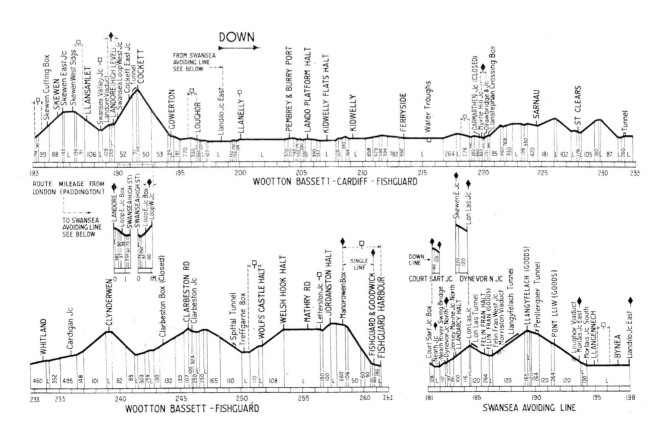

WOOTTON BASSETT – CARDIFF – FISHGUARD

WOOTTON BASSETT – FISHGUARD

SWANSEA AVOIDING LINE

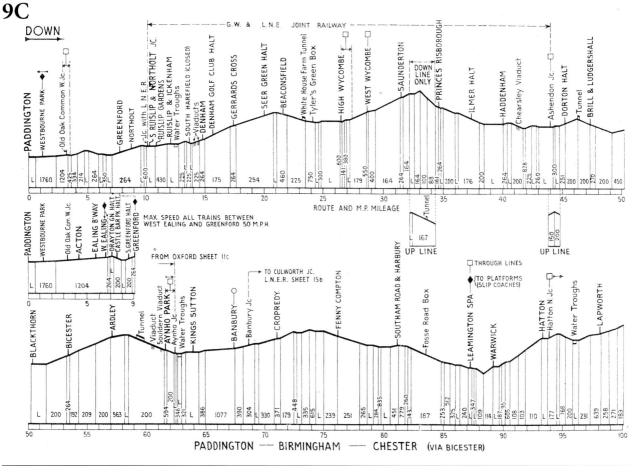

9C

DOWN ▶

PADDINGTON — BIRMINGHAM — CHESTER (VIA BICESTER)

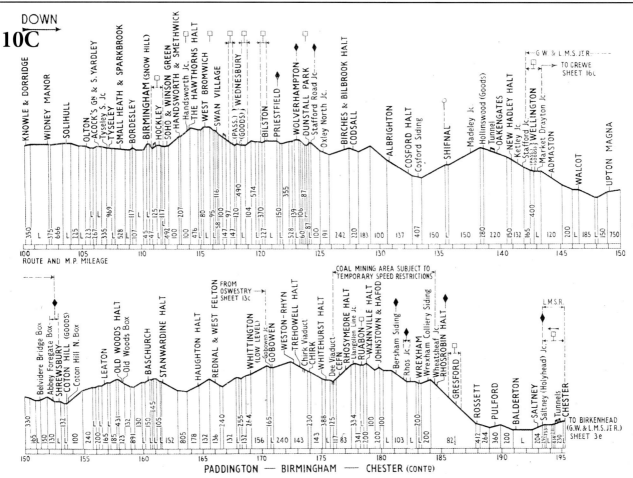

10C

DOWN ▶

ROUTE AND M.P. MILEAGE

PADDINGTON — BIRMINGHAM — CHESTER (CONT?)

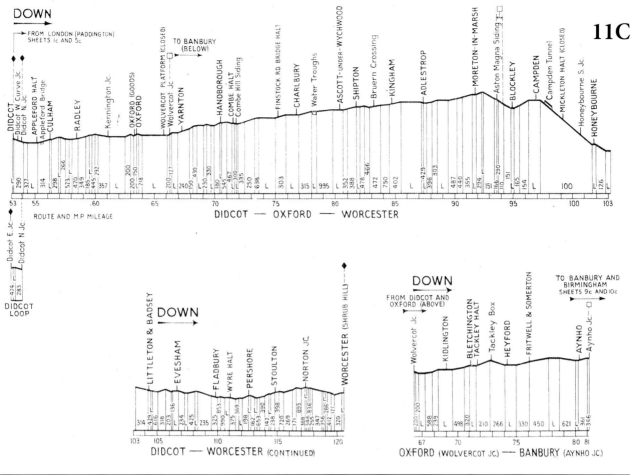

11C

DOWN

→ FROM LONDON (PADDINGTON) SHEETS 1c AND 5c

DIDCOT — OXFORD — WORCESTER

DIDCOT LOOP

DOWN →

DIDCOT — WORCESTER (CONTINUED)

DOWN →

FROM DIDCOT AND OXFORD (ABOVE)

TO BANBURY AND BIRMINGHAM SHEETS 9c AND 10c →

OXFORD (WOLVERCOT JC.) — BANBURY (AYNHO JC.)

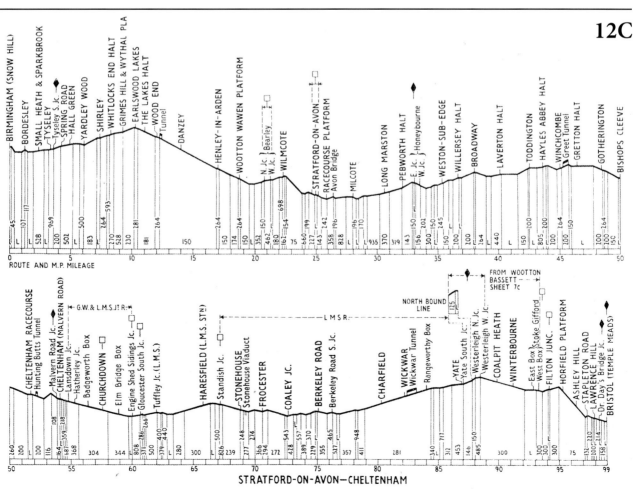

12C

ROUTE AND M.P. MILEAGE

STRATFORD-ON-AVON—CHELTENHAM

13C

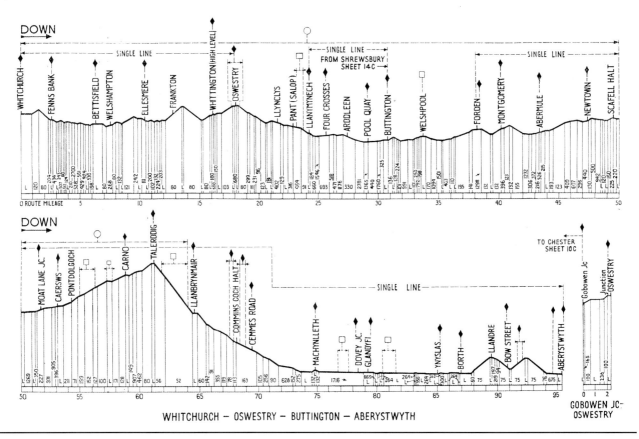

WHITCHURCH — OSWESTRY — BUTTINGTON — ABERYSTWYTH

GOBOWEN JC-
OSWESTRY

14C

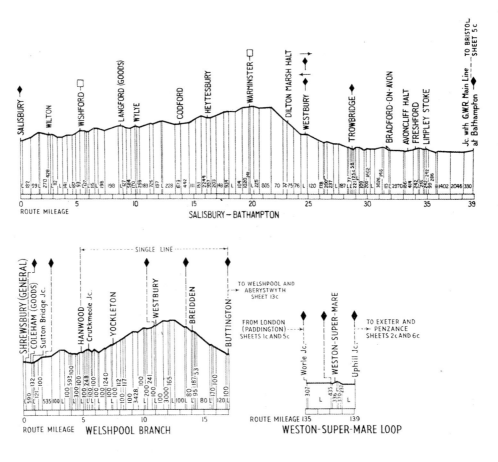

SALISBURY — BATHAMPTON

WELSHPOOL BRANCH

WESTON-SUPER-MARE LOOP

52

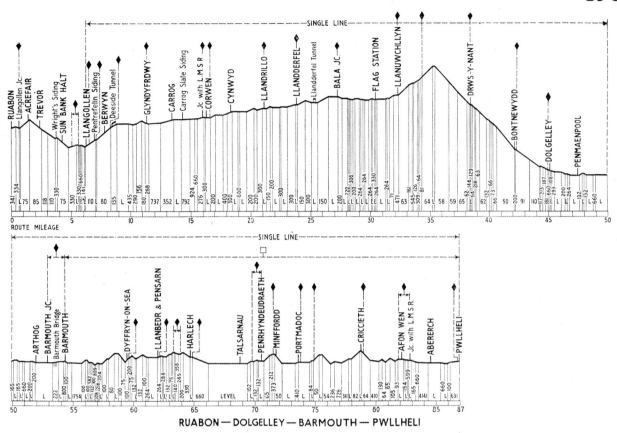

RUABON — DOLGELLEY — BARMOUTH — PWLLHELI

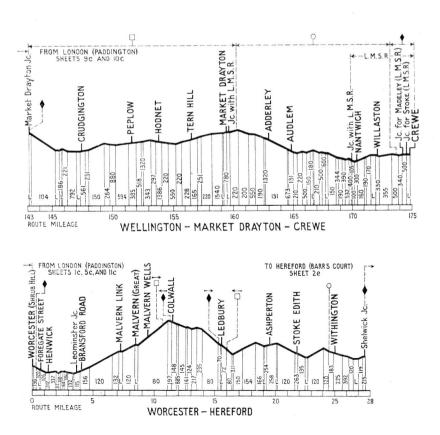

WELLINGTON – MARKET DRAYTON – CREWE

WORCESTER — HEREFORD

Southern Railway

1D

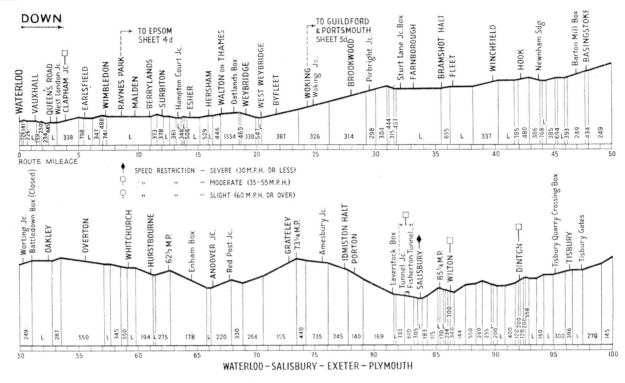

WATERLOO − SALISBURY − EXETER − PLYMOUTH

2D

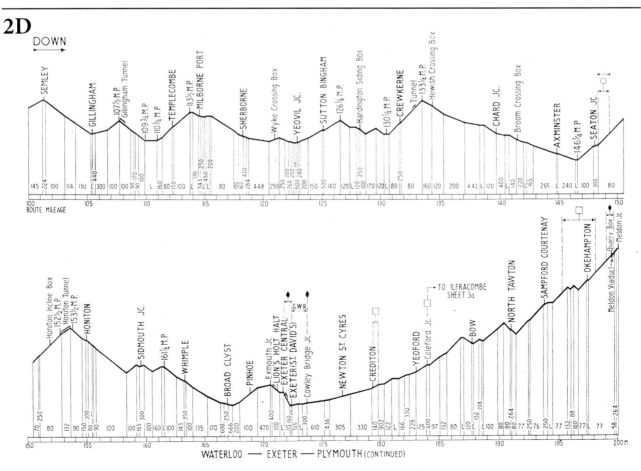

WATERLOO — EXETER — PLYMOUTH (CONTINUED)

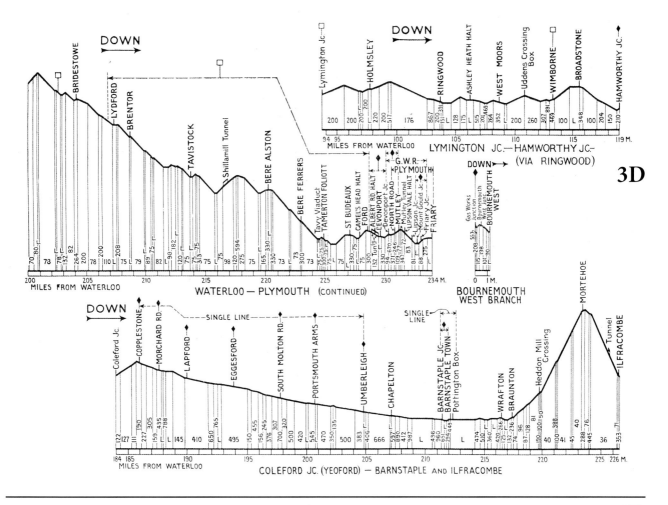

3D

DOWN →

BRIDESTOWE · LYDFORD · BRENTOR · TAVISTOCK · Shillamill Tunnel · BERE ALSTON · BERE FERRERS · Tavy Viaduct · TAMERTON FOLIOTT · ST BUDEAUX · CAMEL'S HEAD HALT · FORD · ALBERT RD HALT · DEVONPORT · NORTH ROAD · MUTLEY · LIPSON VALE HALT · Mutley Tunnel · Lipson Jc · Mount Gould Jc · Friary Jc · FRIARY

G.W.R. PLYMOUTH

MILES FROM WATERLOO
WATERLOO — PLYMOUTH (CONTINUED)

DOWN →

Lymington Jc. · HOLMSLEY · RINGWOOD · ASHLEY HEATH HALT · WEST MOORS · Uddens Crossing Box · WIMBORNE · BROADSTONE · HAMWORTHY JC.

MILES FROM WATERLOO
LYMINGTON JC.—HAMWORTHY JC.—
(VIA RINGWOOD)

DOWN →

Gas Works Junction · Bournemouth West Junc · BOURNEMOUTH WEST

BOURNEMOUTH WEST BRANCH

DOWN →

Coleford Jc. · COPPLESTONE · MORCHARD RD. · LAPFORD · EGGESFORD · SOUTH MOLTON RD · PORTSMOUTH ARMS · UMBERLEIGH · CHAPELTON · BARNSTAPLE JC. · BARNSTAPLE TOWN · Pottington Box · WRAFTON · BRAUNTON · Heddon Mill Crossing · MORTEHOE · Tunnel · ILFRACOMBE

— SINGLE LINE — · SINGLE LINE

MILES FROM WATERLOO
COLEFORD JC. (YEOFORD) — BARNSTAPLE and ILFRACOMBE

4D

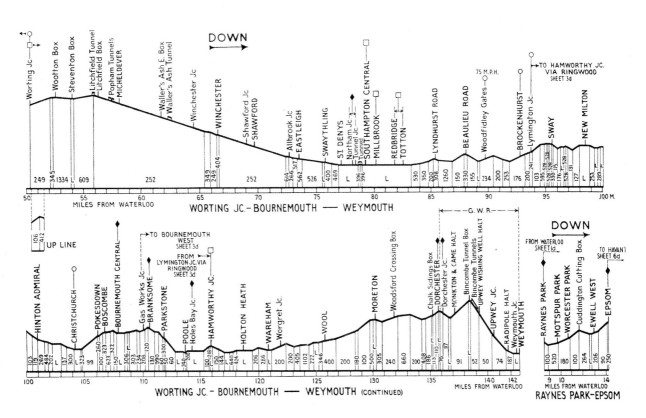

DOWN →

Worting Jc. · Wootton Box · Steventon Box · Litchfield Tunnel · Litchfield Box · Popham Tunnels · MICHELDEVER · Waller's Ash E. Box · Waller's Ash Tunnel · Winchester Jc · WINCHESTER · Shawford Jc · SHAWFORD · Allbrook Jc · EASTLEIGH · SWAYTHLING · ST DENYS · Northam Jc · Tunnel · SOUTHAMPTON CENTRAL · REDBRIDGE · TOTTON · Millbrook · LYNDHURST ROAD · BEAULIEU ROAD · Woodfidley Gates · BROCKENHURST · Lymington Jc · SWAY · NEW MILTON

75 M.P.H.

TO HAMWORTHY JC. VIA RINGWOOD SHEET 3d

MILES FROM WATERLOO
WORTING JC. — BOURNEMOUTH — WEYMOUTH

UP LINE

HINTON ADMIRAL · CHRISTCHURCH · POKESDOWN · BOSCOMBE · BOURNEMOUTH CENTRAL · BRANKSOME · PARKSTONE · Gas Works Jc. · Lymington Jc. · POOLE · Holes Bay Jc. · HAMWORTHY JC. · HOLTON HEATH · WAREHAM · Worgret Jc. · WOOL · MORETON · Woodsford Crossing box · Chalk Sidings Box · DORCHESTER · Dorchester Jc. · MONKTON & CAME HALT · Bincombe Tunnel Box · Bincombe Tunnels · UPWEY WISHING WELL HALT · UPWEY JC. · RADIPOLE HALT · WEYMOUTH

TO BOURNEMOUTH WEST SHEET 3d
FROM LYMINGTON JC. VIA RINGWOOD SHEET 3d

— G.W.R. —

DOWN →

FROM WATERLOO SHEET 1d
TO HAVANT SHEET 6d

RAYNES PARK · MOTSPUR PARK · WORCESTER PARK · Cuddington Cutting Box · EWELL WEST · EPSOM

MILES FROM WATERLOO
WORTING JC. — BOURNEMOUTH — WEYMOUTH (CONTINUED)

MILES FROM WATERLOO
RAYNES PARK-EPSOM

5D

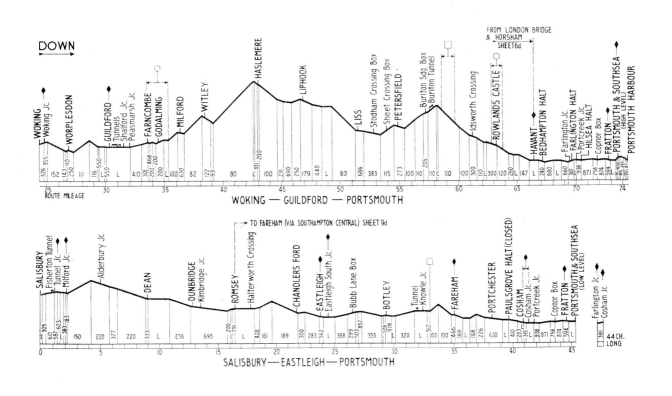

DOWN →

WOKING — GUILDFORD — PORTSMOUTH

SALISBURY — EASTLEIGH — PORTSMOUTH

6D

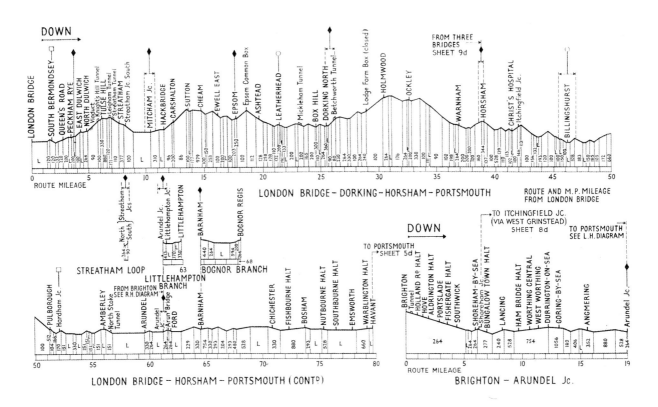

DOWN →

LONDON BRIDGE — DORKING — HORSHAM — PORTSMOUTH

LONDON BRIDGE — HORSHAM — PORTSMOUTH (CONTD)

BRIGHTON — ARUNDEL JC.

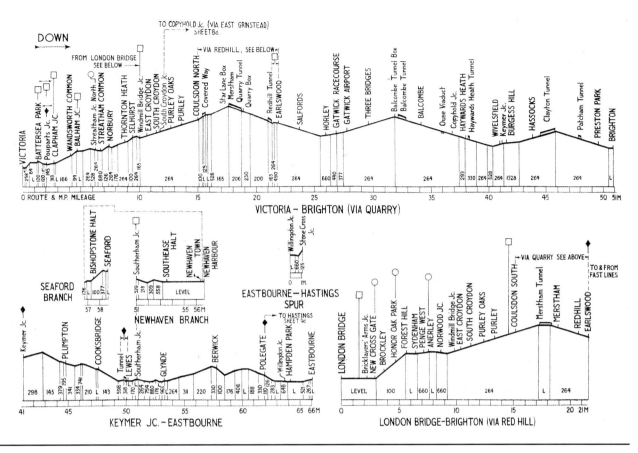

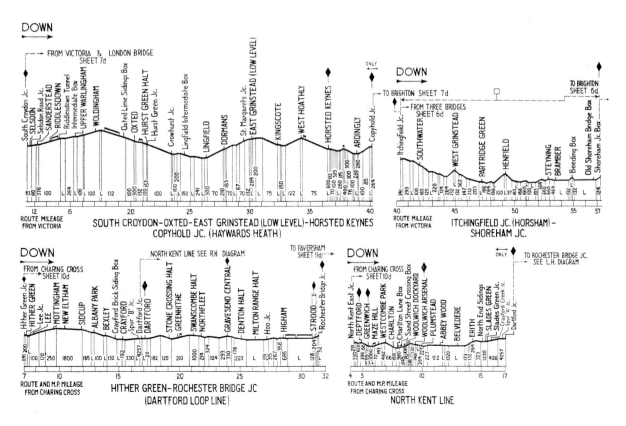

9D

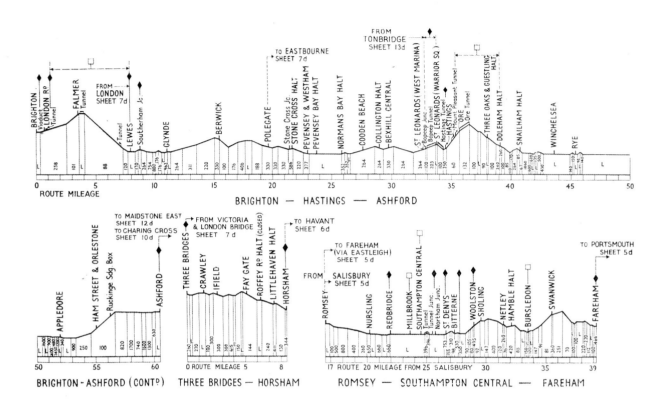

BRIGHTON — HASTINGS — ASHFORD

BRIGHTON-ASHFORD (CONTD)   THREE BRIDGES — HORSHAM   ROMSEY — SOUTHAMPTON CENTRAL — FAREHAM

10D

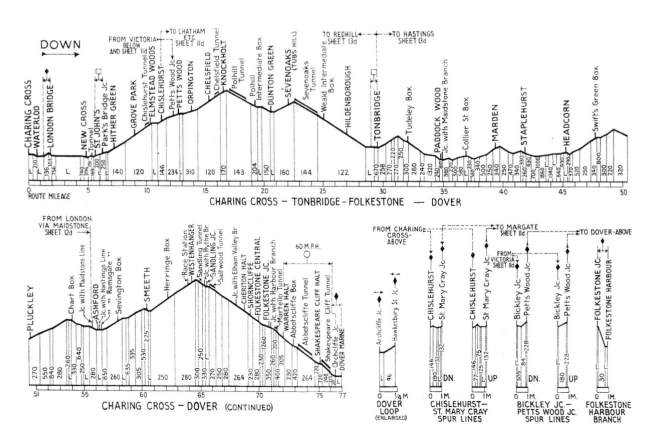

CHARING CROSS — TONBRIDGE — FOLKESTONE — DOVER

CHARING CROSS — DOVER (CONTINUED)

DOVER LOOP (ENLARGED)   CHISLEHURST — ST. MARY CRAY SPUR LINES   BICKLEY JC. — PETTS WOOD JC. SPUR LINES   FOLKESTONE HARBOUR BRANCH

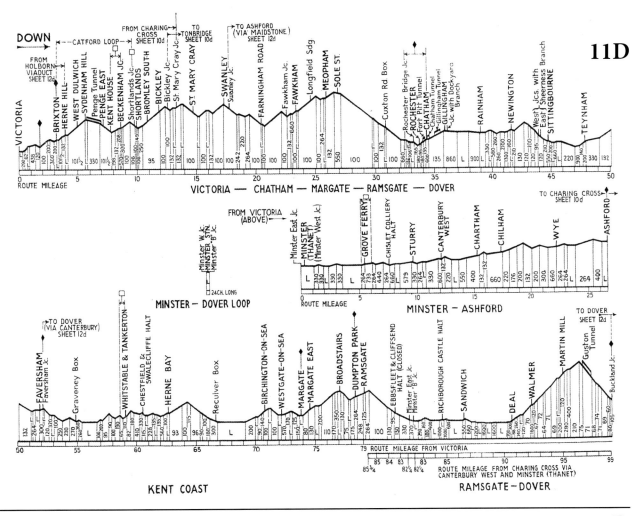

11D

VICTORIA — CHATHAM — MARGATE — RAMSGATE — DOVER

MINSTER — DOVER LOOP

MINSTER — ASHFORD

KENT COAST

RAMSGATE — DOVER

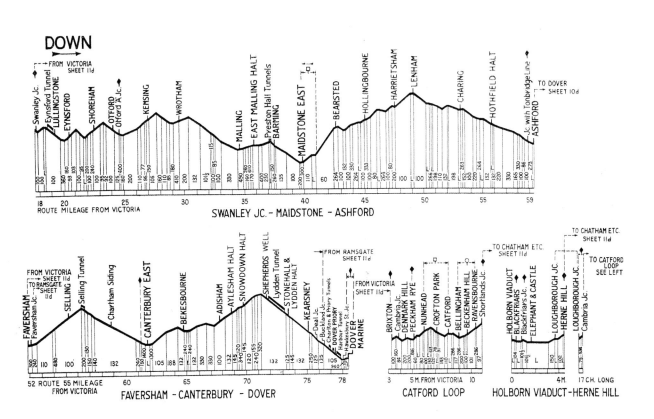

12D

SWANLEY JC. — MAIDSTONE — ASHFORD

FAVERSHAM — CANTERBURY — DOVER

CATFORD LOOP

HOLBORN VIADUCT — HERNE HILL

13D

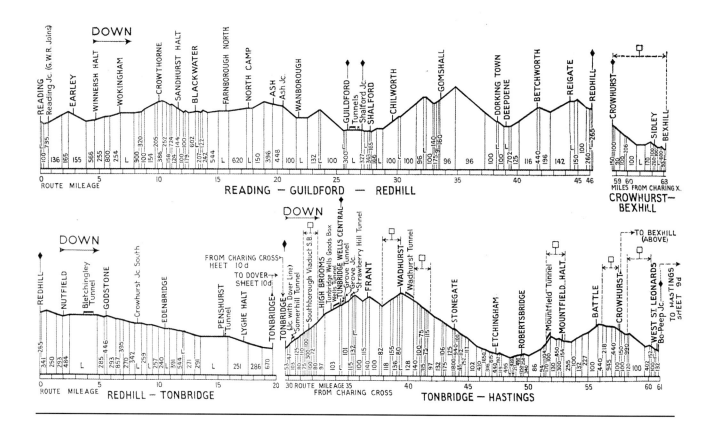

ROUTE MILEAGE
READING — GUILDFORD — REDHILL

CROWHURST— BEXHILL

DOWN

ROUTE MILEAGE
REDHILL — TONBRIDGE

FROM CHARING CROSS

ROUTE MILEAGE
FROM CHARING CROSS
TONBRIDGE — HASTINGS

Joint Lines

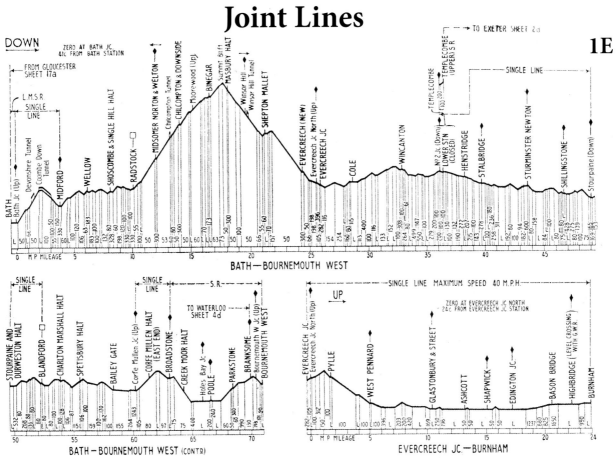

DOWN

ZERO AT BATH JC. 41c FROM BATH STATION

→ TO EXETER SHEET 2a

FROM GLOUCESTER SHEET 17a

L.M.S.R SINGLE LINE

SINGLE LINE

BATH — BOURNEMOUTH WEST

SINGLE LINE

SINGLE LINE

S.R.

TO WATERLOO SHEET 4d

BATH — BOURNEMOUTH WEST (CONTD)

SINGLE LINE MAXIMUM SPEED 40 M.P.H.

UP

ZERO AT EVERCREECH JC NORTH 24c FROM EVERCREECH JC STATION

EVERCREECH JC. — BURNHAM

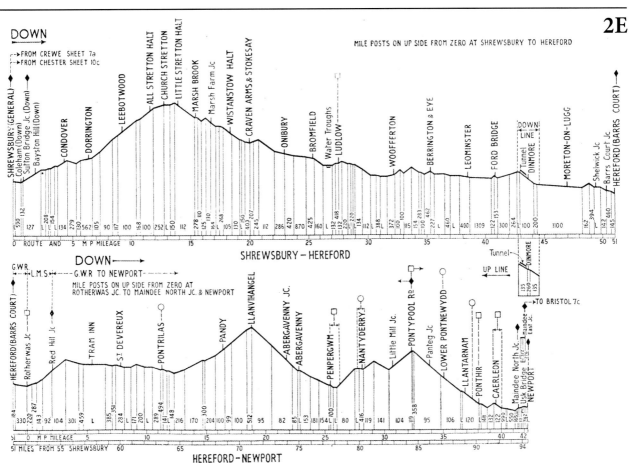

DOWN

FROM CREWE SHEET 7a
FROM CHESTER SHEET 10c

MILE POSTS ON UP SIDE FROM ZERO AT SHREWSBURY TO HEREFORD

DOWN LINE

UP LINE

TO BRISTOL 7c

SHREWSBURY — HEREFORD

DOWN

GWR
LMS

G.W.R. TO NEWPORT

MILE POSTS ON UP SIDE FROM ZERO AT ROTHERWAS JC. TO MAINDEE NORTH JC. & NEWPORT

UP LINE

Tunnel DINMORE

TO BRISTOL 7c

HEREFORD — NEWPORT

MILES FROM SS SHREWSBURY

61

3E

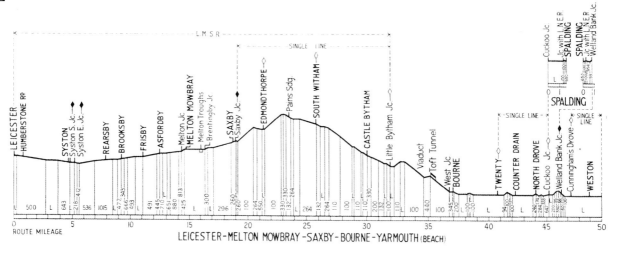

LEICESTER-MELTON MOWBRAY-SAXBY-BOURNE-YARMOUTH (BEACH)

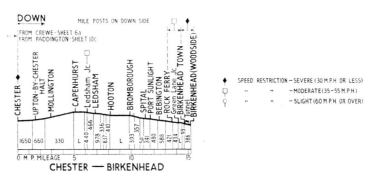

CHESTER — BIRKENHEAD

4E

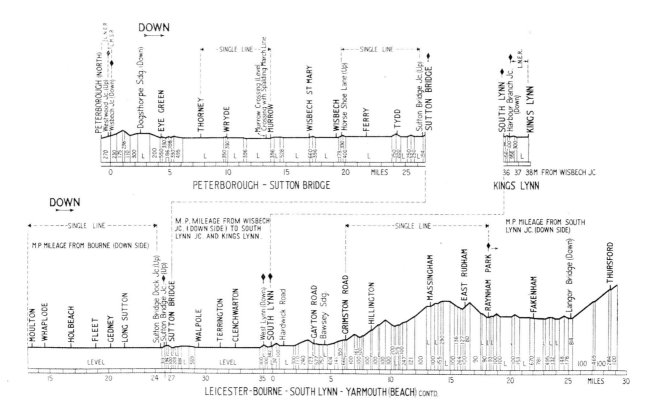

PETERBOROUGH – SUTTON BRIDGE

KINGS LYNN

LEICESTER-BOURNE - SOUTH LYNN - YARMOUTH (BEACH) CONTD.

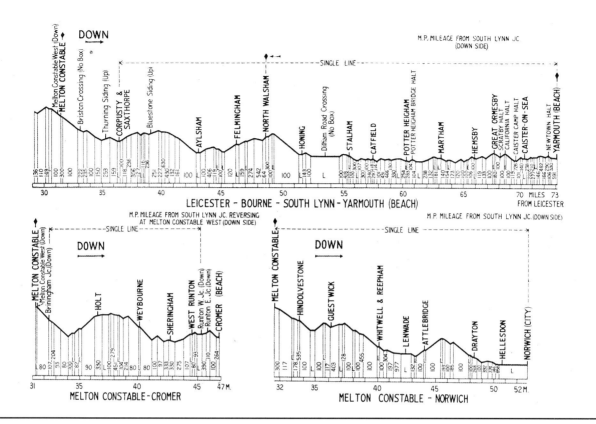

Index

ARDLUI	29B	ASTON-BY-STONE	8A	BALA JNC	15C
ARDSLEY	8B	ATHELNEY	2C	Balavil (Up)	33A
Ardsley (Up)	14A	ATHERSTONE	2A	BALCOMBE	7D
Ardsley Tunnel	14A	ATHERTON	19A	Balcombe Tunnel	7D
ARDWICK	16B	ATTADALE	36A	Balcombe Tunnel Box	7D
Ardwick Jnc	8A	ATTENBOROUGH	16A	BALDERTON	10C
ARISAIG	31B	Attenborough Jnc (Down)	16A	Balderton Box	2B
Arkleston Jnc (Up)	28A, 31A	ATTERCLIFFE ROAD	14A	BALDOCK	5B
ARKSEY	2B	ATTLEBOROUGH	12B	BALHAM JNC	7D
ARKWRIGHT STREET	14B	AUCHENGRAY	28A	BALLATER	28B
ARLESEY	1B	AUCHINDACHY	27B	Ballathie (Down)	26A
ARLEY	18A	AUCHINGATT	32B	BALLINDALLOCH	32B
Arley Colliery Sidings (Up)	18A	AUCHINLECK	29A	BALLINLUIG	32A
ARMATHWAITE	13A	AUCHTERARDER	26A	Ballochmyle Viaduct	29A
Armathwaite Tunnel	13A	AUDENSHAW	8A	Balmanno Jnc	24B
ARMITAGE	2A	AUDLEM	16C	BALNE	2B
ARMLEY	11A, 20A, 8B	AUDLEY END	11B	BALQUHIDDER	38A
ARNAGE	32B	AUGHTON PARK	23A	Balquhidder Jnc	38A
ARROCHAR & TARBET	29B	AULDBAR ROAD	26A	BALSHAW LANE	3A
ARTHINGTON	8B	AULDEARN	34A	Balsporran (Up)	33A
ARTHOG	15C	AULDGIRTH	29A	BAMBER BRIDGE	23A
Arun Bridge Ford	6D	AUTHORPE	5B	Bamber Bridge Jnc (Up)	23A
ARUNDEL	6D	AVIEMORE	33A, 34A	BAMFORD	15A
Arundel Jnc	6D	Avon Bridge	12C	BAMFURLONG	2A
ASCOT-UNDER-WYCHWOOD	11C	Avon Viaduct	17A	BANAVIE	31B
Asfordby Tunnel	14A	AVONCLIFF HALT	14C	Banavie Jnc	31B
ASH	13D	Awe Crossing	38A	BANBURY	15B, 9C
Ash Jnc	13D	AWRE JNC	6C	Banbury Jnc	15B, 9C
Ashburton Jnc	3C	AXMINSTER	2D	Banbury Lane (Down)	1A
ASHBURYS	16B	AYCLIFFE	3B	BANCHORY	28B
ASHBY MAGNA	13B	AYLESBURY	13B	Bangor Tunnel	6A
ASHCHURCH	17A	AYLESHAM HALT	12D	BANK HALL	20A
ASHCOTT	1E	AYNHO	11C	Bankhouse Tunnel	20A
Ashendon Jnc	15B, 9C	Aynho Jnc	9C, 11C	BANNOCKBURN	26A
ASHFORD	9D, 10D, 12D	AYNHO PARK	9C	BARASSIE	31A
ASHLEY HEATH HALT	3D	AYR	31A	BARDON MILL	22B
ASHLEY HILL	12C	AYTON	4B	BARDSEY	8B
ASHPERTON	16C	Badgeworth (Down)	17A	Bargany (Down)	31A
ASHTEAD	6D	Badgeworth Box	12C	BARKING	18A
ASHTON-UNDER-LYNE	9A	BADMINTON	7C	BARKSTON	2B
ASHWELL	14A, 5B	Badnall Wharf (Down)	2A	BARLASTON	8A
ASKERN	19B	BAGILLT	6A	Barlby Jnc	18B
Askham Tunnel	2B	Bagthorpe Jnc	14B	BARMING	12D
Astbury Sidings (Down)	8A	BAGULEY	16B	BARMOUTH	15C
ASTLEY	9A	BAILEY GATE	1E	Barmouth Bridge	15C
Astley Bridge Jnc (Down)	21A	BAILIFF BRIDGE (CLOSED)	23A	BARMOUTH JNC	15C
ASTON	5A, 7A	BAINTON	18B	BARNBY DUN	20B
Aston Magna Siding	11C	BAKEWELL	15A	BARNBY MOOR	2B

BARNETBY	23B	Bearley W Jnc	12C	BENTHAM	18A
BARNHAM	6D	BEARSTED	12D	BENTLEY	9B
Barnsley Jnc	14B	BEASDALE	31B	Benton Bank Box	3B
BARNSTAPLE JNC	3D	BEATTOCK	24A	BERE ALSTON	3D
BARNSTAPLE TOWN	3D	BEAUCHIEF	14A	BERE FERRERS	3D
Barnston Box	14B	BEAULIEU ROAD	4D	BERKELEY ROAD	17A, 12C
BARNT GREEN	17A	BEAULY	35A	Berkeley Road S Jnc	17A, 12C
Baron Wood Tunnels	13A	BECCLES	10B, 12B	BERKSWELL & BALSALL COMMON	4A
Barony Jnc (Up)	29A	Beccles Bank Box	10B	Bernhill (Up)	27A
BARRHEAD	30A	Beccles Swing Bridge	10B	BERRINGTON & EYE	2E
BARRHILL	31A	BECKENHAM HILL	12D	BERRY BROW	23A
BARROW HILL & STAVELEY		BECKENHAM JNC	11D	BERRYLANDS	1D
WORKS	11A	BECKINGHAM	7B	Bersham Siding	10C
BARROW-ON-SOAR	11A	BECONTREE	18A	BERWICK	4B, 7D, 9D
Barrs Court Jnc	2E	Bedford N. Jnc (Up)	10A	BERWYN	15C
BARRY LINKS	26B	BEDHAMPTON HALT	5D	BESCAR LANE	20A
BARTON & BROUGHTON		BEDMINSTER	5C	BESCOT	7A
(CLOSED)	3A	BEDWYN	1C	BETCHWORTH	13D
BARTON & WALTON	16A	Beechwood Tunnel	4A	Betchworth Tunnel	6D
BARTON HILL	19B	Beeding Box	8D	BETHNAL GREEN	11B
Barton Mill Box	1D	BEESTON	16A, 8B	BETLEY ROAD	2A
Barton Moss Jnc (Down)	9A	BEESTON CASTLE	6A	BETTISFIELD	13C
BASCHURCH	10C	Beeston N Jnc (Down)	16A	BEVERLEY	20B
Basford Sand Sidings (Down)	2A	BEIGHTON	14B	Beverley Jnc	20B
Basford Wood (Down)	2A	Beighton Jnc (Up)	11A	BEXHILL	13D
Basildon East (Down)	18A	BEITH (NORTH)	31A	BEXHILL CENTRAL	9D
Basildon West (Down)	18A	BEKESBOURNE	12D	BEXLEY	8D
BASINGSTOKE	4C, 1D	BELFORD	4B	BICESTER	9C
BASON BRIDGE	1E	BELGRAVE	14B	BICKLEY	11D
BATH	17A, 5C, 1E	BELL BUSK	12A	Bickley Jnc	10D, 11D
Bath Jnc (Up)	17A, 1E	BELLAHOUSTON	31A	Big Fleet Viaduct	30A
BATHAMPTON	5C	BELLINGHAM	12D	BIGGLESWADE	1B
BATHFORD HALT	5C	BELLSHILL	28A	BILBSTER	37A
BATTERSEA PARK	7D	Bellwater Jnc	5B	BILLERICAY	12B
BATTLE	13D	Belmont (Down)	31A	BILLINGHAM-ON-TEES	17B
Battledown Box (Closed)	1D	Belmont Tunnel	6A	BILLINGSHURST	6D
Batty Moss Viaduct	12A	BELPER	15A	BILSTON	10C
BAWTRY	2B	BELSES	21B	Bilton Road	17B
BAXENDEN	23A	BELTON	10B	Bincombe Tunnel	4C, 4D
BAY HORSE	3A	Beltonford Siding	4B	Bincombe Tunnel Box	4C, 4D
BAYFORD	22B	BELVEDERE	8D	BINEGAR	1E
Bayston Hill (Down)	2E	Belvidere Bridge Box	10C	BINGLEY	12A
Beacon Hill Tunnel	20A	BEMPTON	20B	Bingley Jnc (Down)	12A
BEACONSFIELD	15B, 9C	BENFLEET	18A	Bingley Tunnel	12A
BEAL	4B	Benhar Jnc (Up)	28A	BIRCHES & BILBROOK HALT	10C
BEALINGS	10B	BENINGBROUGH	2B	BIRCHFIELD HALT	27B
BEANACRE HALT	4C	Bennerley Jnc (Down)	11A	BIRCHINGTON-ON-SEA	11D
Bearley N Jnc	12C	BENSHAM	3B	Birdswood (Between)	7A

Birdswood (Down)	2A	BLISWORTH	1A	Bow Jnc	9B
BIRKDALE	20A	BLOCKLEY	11C	BOW STREET	13C
Birkelt Tunnel	13A	Bloomfield Road (Down)	22A	BOWBRIDGE CROSSING HALT	6C
BIRMINGHAM (NEW ST)	5A, 7A, 17A	BLOWICK (CLOSED)	20A	BOWER	36A
BIRMINGHAM (SNOW HILL)	10C, 12C	BLUNDELL SANDS & CROSBY	20A	BOWES PARK	22B
BIRTLEY	3B	BLYTON FOR CORRINGHAM	23B	Bowhouse (Up)	29A
BISHOPBRIGGS	24B	BOAR'S HEAD	2A	BOWLAND	21B
BISHOPS CLEEVE	12C	BOAT OF GARTEN	34A, 32B	BOWLING	28B
BISHOPS STORTFORD	11B	BODMIN ROAD	3C	Bowling (Up)	20A
BISHOPSTONE HALT	7D	BODORGAN	6A	BOWLING JNC	20A
BISHOPTON	28A	Bodorgan Tunnels	6A	BOX HILL	6D
Bishopton Tunnels	28A	BOGART	35A	Brackenhill Jnc	29A, 15B
BITTAFORD PLATFORM	3C	BOGSIDE	31A	BRACKLEY	13B
BITTERNE	9D	BOGSTON	28A	BRADBURY	3B
BITTON	17A	BOLDON COLLIERY	17B	BRADFIELD	12B
BLABY	18A	BOLTON	22A	BRADFORD	20A
Blachford Viaduct	3C	BOLTON (TRINITY ST)	21A	BRADFORD (EXCHANGE)	8B
BLACK BANK	6B	Bolton Jnc (Up)	21A, 23A	BRADFORD PEVERALL &	
Black Carr Jnc	7B	BOLTON PERCY	19B	STRATTON HALT	4C
Black Rock (Up)	9A	BOLTON-LE-SANDS	3A	Bradford S Jnc	4C
BLACKBURN	21A, 23A	BOLTON-ON-DEARNE	15B	BRADFORD-ON-AVON	14C
Blackett Colliery Box	22B	BONAR BRIDGE	35A	Bradkirk (Down)	22A
BLACKFORD	26A	BONNY BRIDGE	24B	Bradkirk (Up)	22A
BLACKFRIARS	12D	Bonnymuir (Up)	26A	BRADLEY	23A
Blackfriars Jnc	12D	BONTNEWYDD	15C	Bradley Wood Jnc (Down)	19A
BLACKHALL COLLIERY	17B	Bootham Jnc	20B	Bradley Wood Jnc (Up)	23A
BLACKHALL ROCKS	17B	BOOTLE (ORIEL ROAD)	20A	Bradway Tunnel	14A
BLACKPOOL (CENTRAL)	22A	Bopeep Juc	9D, 13D	BRAIDWOOD	25A
BLACKPOOL (NORTH)	21A	Bopeep Tunnel	9D	BRAMBER	8D
BLACKPOOL (SOUTH)	22A	Border Counties Box	22B	BRAMFORD	9B
BLACKROD	22A	BORDESLEY	10C, 12C	BRAMHALL	8A
BLACKSBOAT	32B	Bordesley Jnc (Down)	16A	Bramhall Moor Lane (Down)	15A
BLACKTHORN	9C	BORROBOL PLATFORM	36A	Bramhope Tunnel	8B
BLACKWATER	13D	BORROWASH	15A	BRAMLEY	20A, 8B
BLACKWELL	17A	BORTH	13C	BRAMLEY (for SILCHESTER)	4C
Bladenoch Viaduct	30A	Borthwick Bank	21B	BRAMPTON (SUFFOLK)	10B
BLAIR ATHOLL	32A	BOSCOMBE	4D	BRAMPTON JUNCTION	22B
BLAIRADAM (CLOSED)	24B	BOSHAM	6D	BRAMSHOT HALT	1D
BLANDFORD	1E	BOSTON	5B	Brancliffe East Jnc (Down)	16B
BLANKNEY	6B	BOTLEY	5D	BRANDON	11B
BLAYDON	22B	Botriphnie Siding	27B	BRANDON & WOLSTON	4A
Blea Moor (Up)	12A	BOTT LANE HALT	23A	Brandon Ballast Pit (Down)	4A
Blea Moor Tunnel	12A	Boultham Crossing	16A	Brandord N Jnc	4C
BLEADON & UPHILL	6C	BOURNEMOUTH CENTRAL	4D	BRANKSOME	4D, 1E
BLEASBY	16A	BOURNEMOUTH WEST	3D, 1E	BRANSFORD ROAD	16C
Bletchingley Tunnel	13D	Bournemouth West Jnc	3D, 1E	BRANSTON	6B
BLETCHINGTON	11C	BOURNVILLE	17A	BRANSTON (CLOSED)	16A
BLETCHLEY	1A	BOW	2D	Branston Jnc (Up)	16A

Brassey (Up)	6A	BRITON FERRY (WEST)	7C	BUCKIE	27B
BRAUNSTON	13B	Brittania Tubular Bridge	6A	Buckingham Jnc (Down)	27A
BRAUNTON	3D	BRIXTON	11D, 12D	Buckland Jnc	11D, 12D
Braybrook (Up)	10A	BROAD CLYST	2D	BUCKPOOL	27B
BREAN ROAD PLATFORM	6C	BROAD GREEN	9A	BUCKSBURN	26B, 32B
Bredbury Jnc	16B	Broadholme (Down)	15A	Buckshead Tunnel	3C
BREDON	17A	BROADSTAIRS	11D	BULKINGTON (closed)	1A
BREICH	28A	BROADSTONE	3D, 1E	Bullfield West (Down)	22A
BREIDDEN	14C	BROADWAY	12C	Bullo Pill Jnc & Goods	6C
BRENT	3C	BROCK (CLOSED)	3A	BULWELL COMMON	14B
Brent Jc (Up)	1A	Brock Troughs	3A	BUNCHREW	35A
Brent Jnc No 1 (Up)	10A	BROCKENHURST	4D	BUNGALOW TOWN HALT	6D
BRENT KNOLL	6C	BROCKHOLES	23A	Burbage Siding	1C
Brentingby Jnc (Down)	14A	BROCKLESBY	23B	BURDETT ROAD	18A
BRENTOR	3D	BROCKLEY	7D	BURGESS HILL	7D
BRENTWOOD	9B	BRODIE	34A	BURGH-LE-MARSH	5B
Brewham Box	2C	BROMFIELD	2E	Buriton Siding Box	5D
Brick Kiln Lane Crossing	7A	BROMFORD BRIDGE (CLOSED)	16A	Buriton Tunnel	5D
Bricklayer's Arms Jnc	7D	Bromham (Up)	10A	BURLESDON	9D
BRIDESTOWE	3D	BROMLEY	18A	BURLINGTON ROAD HALT	22A
BRIDGE OF ALLAN	26A	BROMLEY CROSS	21A	BURN MAZE HALT	22A
BRIDGE OF DUN	27A	BROMLEY SOUTH	11D	BURNAGE	8A
BRIDGE OF EARN	24B	BROMPTON	17B	Burnden Jnc (Down)	22A
BRIDGE OF ORCHY	29B	BROMSGROVE	17A	BURNGULLOW	3C
BRIDGE OF WEIR	30A	Brookbottom Tunnel	23A	BURNHAM	1E
BRIDGEND	7C	BROOKMANS PARK	1B	BURNHAM (BUCKS)	1C
BRIDGEND FACTORY HALT		BROOKWOOD	1D	BURNLEY	23A
(CLOSED)	7C	Broom Crossing Box	2D	BURNLEY (CENTRAL)	23A
BRIDGWATER	6C	BROOMFLEET	18B	BURNLEY BARRACKS	23A
BRIDLINGTON	18B, 20B	BROOMHILL	34A	BURNMOUTH	4B
BRIERFIELD	23A	Broomhouse Tunnel	14A	BURNT HILL	11B
BRIGG	23B	BRORA	35A	BURNT ISLAND	25B
BRIGHOUSE	19A	BROUGH	18B	BURRELTON	26A
BRIGHTON	6D, 7D, 9D	BROUGHTON GIFFORD HALT	4C	Burscough Abbey (Down)	23A
BRIGHTON ROAD	16A	BROUGHTON LANE	15B	BURSCOUGH BRIDGE	20A
BRIGHTSIDE	14A	BROUGHTY FERRY	26B	BURSCOUGH JNC	23A
BRILL & LUDGERSHALL	9C	Brownhill Jnc (Down)	31A	Burscough N Jnc (Down)	23A
BRIMSCOMBE	6C	Brownqueen Tunnel	3C	Burscough S Jnc (Down)	23A
BRIMSCOMBE BRIDGE HALT	6C	BROXBOURNE	11B	BURSTON	9B
BRIMSDOWN	11B	Broxbourne Jnc	11B	BURTON & HOLME	3A
BRINKLOW	1A	Broxburn Jnc	32A	BURTON AGNES	18B
BRINKWORTH	7C	BRUCKLAY	32B	BURTON JOYCE	16A
Brinnington Jnc (Down)	16B	Bruern Crossing	11C	BURTON LATIMER	10A
Brinnington Tunnel	16B	BRUNSWICK (DOWN)	16B	BURTON SALMON	19A, 15B, 19B
Brislington Tunnel	5C	BRUTON	2C	BURTON-ON-TRENT	16A
BRISTOL (TEMPLE MEADS)		BRYN-Y-GWYNON (GOODS)	7C	BURY (BOLTON ST)	23A
	17A, 5C, 12C	Bubb Lane Box	5D	Bury Loco Jnc (Up)	23A
Bristol East Depot	5C	BUBWITH	18B	BURY ST EDMUNDS	7B

Bury Tunnel	23A	Cardigan Jnc	8C	CASTLE HOWARD	19B
Busby Jnc (Up)	30A	CARDONALD	28A, 31A	CASTLE KENNEDY	31A
Bushbury No 1 (Down)	5A, 7A	CARDROSS	28B	CASTLE STUART HALT	34A
BUSHEY & OXHEY	1A	CARFIN HALT	28A	CASTLECARY	24B
Bushey Troughs	1A	CARGILL	26A	Castlecary (Down)	26A
BUTTINGTON	13C, 14C	CARLISLE	3A, 21B	CASTLEFORD	19A
BUXWORTH	15A	CARLISLE (CITADEL)	14A, 24A	Castlehill (Down)	25A
Buxworth Jnc (Down)	15A	CARLISLE (LMSR)	22B	Castlemilk (Closed – Up)	24A
BYFLEET	1D	Carlisle No 13 (Down)	3A	CASTLETHORPE	1A
BYNEA	8C	Carlisle No 3 (Up)	24A	Castlethorpe Troughs	1A
Byrehill Jnc (Down)	31A	CARLTON & NETHERFIELD	16A	CASTLETON	19A
CADISHEAD	16B	CARLTON-ON-TRENT	2B	Castleton E Jnc (Down)	19A
CAERLEON	2E	CARLUKE	25A	Castleton S Jnc (Up)	19A
CAERSWS	13C	CARMARTHEN JNC (CLOSED)	8C	Catesby Tunnel	13B
Cairn Ryon Jnc (Down)	31A	CARMONT	27A	CATFORD	12D
Cairn Valley Jnc (Down)	29A	CARMOUNT	26B	CATON	18A
Cairnie Jnc	27B	Carmuirs E Jnc	32A	Cattybrook Siding	7C
CAIRNIE JUNCTION	27B	Carmuirs W Jnc (Up)	26A	CAYTON	20B
Calcot Box	1C	CARN BREA	3C	CEFN	10C
CALCOTS	27B	CARNABY	18B	Cemetery Hill Siding (Up)	21A
Calder Viaduct	27A	CARNFORTH	3A	Cemetery N Jnc	17B
CALDWELL	30A	CARNO	13C	Cemetery W Jnc	17B
CALLANDER	38A	CARNOUSTIE	26B	CEMMES ROAD	13C
CALTHWAITE	3A	CARNWATH	28A	CHACEWATER	3C
CALVELEY	6A	CARPENDER'S PARK	1A	Chaddesden S Jnc (Down)	15A
CALVERLEY & RODLEY	12A	CARR BRIDGE	33A	CHADWELL HEATH	9B
CALVERT	13B	CARROG	15C	CHALCOMBE ROAD HALT	15B
CAMBORNE	3C	Carrog Slate Siding	15C	CHALFONT	13B
Cambria Jnc	12D	CARRON	32B	Chalk Sidings Box	4D
CAMBRIDGE	7B, 11B	CARRONBRIDGE	29A	CHALKWELL	18A
CAMBRIDGE HEATH	11B	CARSHALTON	6D	Challoch Jnc	30A
CAMBUS	28B	CARSTAIRS	25A, 28A	Challoch Jnc (No box)	31A
CAMBUSLANG	25A	Cart Jnc (Down)	31A	CHALLOW	5C
Camden No 1 (Up)	1A	CARTLY	27B	Chaloner Whin Jnc	2B, 19B
CAMEL'S HEAD HALT	3D	Cartsburn Jnc (Down)	30A	CHANDLERS FORD	5D
CAMELON	32A	Cartsburn Tunnel	28A	CHAPEL-EN-LE-FRITH	15A
CAMP HILL (CLOSED)	16A	CARTSDYKE	28A	CHAPELTON	3D
CAMPDEN	11C	Carwardine Cutting (Up)	2A	CHAPELTOWN	14A
Campden Tunnel	11C	CASHES GREEN HALT	6C	CHARD JNC	2D
Camperdown Jnc	25B	CASSILIS	31A	CHARFIELD	17A, 12C
Canal Jnc	21B	CASTLE BAR PK HALT	9C	CHARING	12D
Canfield Place Box	13B	CASTLE BROMWICH	16A	CHARING CROSS	10D
Canklow Goods Jnc (Down)	11A	CASTLE CARY	2C, 4C	CHARLBURY	11C
CANLEY HALT	4A	Castle Cary Jnc	2C, 4C	CHARLTON	8D
CANTERBURY EAST	12D	CASTLE DOUGLAS	30A	Charlton & Priory Tunnels	12D
Canton Crossing Box	7C	CASTLE GRANT HALT	34A	Charlton Lane Box	8D
CARCROFT	8B	Castle Hill Tunnel	19A	CHARLTON MACKRELL	2C
CARDIFF (GENERAL)	7C	Castle Hills	8B	CHARLTON MARSHALL HALT	1E

Chart Box	10D	Chinley E Jnc (Down)	15A	CLAYPOLE	2B
Chartham Siding	12D	Chinley N Jnc (Down)	15A	CLAYTON BRIDGE	9A
CHARWELTON	13B	Chinley S Jnc (Up)	15A	Clayton Tunnel	7D
CHASSEN ROAD	16B	CHIPPENHAM	5C	CLECKHEATON	20A
CHATBURN	21A	Chippenham Jnc	7B	CLEETHORPES	23B
CHATHAM	11D	CHIPPING SODBURY	7C	CLEEVE	17A
Chatham Tunnel	11D	CHIRK	10C	CLEGHORN	25A
CHATHILL	4B	Chirk Viaduct	10C	CLELAND	28A
CHATTERLEY	8A	CHISLEHURST	10D	Cliff Colliery Siding (Up)	16A
CHEADLE	16B	Chislehurst Tunnel	10D	CLIFF COMMON	18B
CHEADLE HEATH	15A	CHOLSEY & MOULSFORD	5C	CLIFTON & LOWTHER (CLOSED)	3A
CHEADLE HULME	8A	CHORLEY	22A	CLIFTON JNC	22A, 23A
Cheadle Jnc (Up)	16B	Chorley Tunnel	22A	Clifton Maybank Jnc	4C
CHEAM	6D	CHORLEY WOOD	13B	CLIFTON ROAD (CLOSED)	23A
Chearsley Viaduct	15B, 9C	Chorlton Jnc	15A, 16B	Clinnick Viaduct	3C
CHECKER HOUSE (CLOSED)	16B	CHORLTON-CUM-HARDY	15A, 16B	CLITHEROE	21A
Chee Tor Tunnels	15A	CHRIST'S HOSPITAL	6D	Cliviger East (Up)	23A
Cheetham Hill Jnc (Down)	19A	CHRISTCHURCH	4D	CLOCKSBRIGGS	26A
CHELFORD	8A	CHRISTIAN MALFORD HALT	5C	CLOSEBURN	29A
Chelford Loop (Down)	8A	Christleton (Up)	6A	CLUNES	35A
Chelford Sidings (Down)	8A	Christleton Tunnel	6A	Clyde Viaduct	25A
CHELMSFORD	9B	CHRISTON BANK	4B	CLYNDERWEN	8C
CHELSFIELD	10D	CHURCH & OSWALDTWISTLE	23A	COALEY JNC	17A, 12C
Chelsfield Tunnel	10D	CHURCH BRAMPTON (Closed)	4A	COALPIT HEATH	7C, 12C
CHELTENHAM (LANSDOWN)	17A	CHURCH FENTON	19A, 15B, 19B	COATBRIDGE	26A
CHELTENHAM (MALVERN ROAD)	12C	Church Road Jnc (Down)	17A	COATES (GOODS)	6C
CHELTENHAM RACECOURSE	12C	CHURCH STRETTON	2E	Coates Pk N (Up)	11A
CHEPSTOW	6C	CHURCHDOWN	17A, 12C	COBBINSHAW	28A
CHERITON HALT	10D	CHURSTON	4C	COCKBURNSPATH	4B
CHERRY BURTON	20B	City Basin Jnc	2C	COCKETT	8C
CHERRY TREE	23A	Clachnaharry (Closed)	35A	Cockett East Jnc	8C
CHESHUNT	11B	CLACTON-ON-SEA	12B	CODFORD	14C
CHESTER	6A, 7A, 10C	CLAPHAM	18A	CODNOR PARK	11A
Chester Water Troughs	6A	CLAPHAM JNC	1D, 7D	CODSALL	10C
CHESTER-LE-STREET	3B	CLAPTON	11B	Cogload Jnc	2C, 6C
CHESTERFIELD	11A	Clapton Jnc	11B	COLCHESTER	9B, 12B
Chesterton Jnc	11B	Clara Vale Box	22B	Coldham Lane Jnc	7B
CHESTFIELD & SWALECLIFFE HALT	11D	Clarbeston Box (Closed)	8C	Coldrenick Viaduct	3C
		Clarbeston Jnc	8C	COLE	1E
CHETNOLE HALT	4C	CLARBESTON ROAD	8C	Coleburn Siding	27B
CHETTISHAM	6B	Clarborough Jnc	6B, 23B	Coleford Jnc	2D, 3D
CHEVINGTON	3B	Clarborough Tunnel	6B	Coleham (Down)	2E
CHICHESTER	6D	Claughton Manor (Up)	18A	COLEHAM (GOODS)	14C
CHILCOMPTON & DOWNSIDE	1E	CLAY CROSS	11A, 16A	COLESHILL	18A
Chilcompton Tunnel	1E	Clay Cross S Jnc	11A, 16A	Collier St Box	10D
CHILTERN GREEN	10A	Clay Cross Tunnel	16A	COLLINGHAM	16A
CHILWORTH	13D	Clay Mills Jnc (Down)	16A	COLLINGHAM BRIDGE	8B
CHINLEY	15A	CLAYDON	9B	COLLINGTON HALT	9D

COLLINS GREEN	9A
COLNE	23A
COLWALL	16C
COLWICH	2A, 8A
COLWYN BAY	6A
COMBE HALT	11C
Combe Hill Siding	11C
COMMINS COCH HALT	13C
CONDOVER	2E
CONGLETON	8A
Congleton Viaduct	8A
CONISBOROUGH	22B
CONNAHS QUAY	6A
Connahs Quay No 1 (Up)	6A
CONNEL FERRY	38A
Connel Ferry Jnc	38A
Connington Box	1B
CONON	35A
CONONLEY	12A
CONWAY	6A
Conway Bridge	6A
Conway Morfa (Up)	6A
COODEN BEACH	9D
COOKSBRIDGE	7D
Coombe Down Tunnel	1E
Coombe Viaduct	3C
COOPER BRIDGE	19A
Copenhagen Tunnel	1B
COPLEY (CLOSED)	20A
COPMANTHORPE	19B
Copnor Box	5D
Coppenhall Jc (Up)	2A
Copper Mills Jnc	11B
COPPLESTONE	3D
COPPULL	2A
Coppull Hall Siding (Down)	2A
Copy Pit Siding (Up)	23A
Copyhold Jnc	7D, 8D
CORBRIDGE	22B
Corbridge Tunnel	22B
CORBY	1B
CORBY & WELDON	14A
Corby Tunnel	14A
Cordio Jnc	17B
CORFE MULLEN HALT (EAST END)	1E
Corfe Mullen Jnc	1E
CORKERHILL	31A
Cornbrook W Jnc (Down)	16B

Cornbrook W Jnc (Up)	15A
CORNHILL	27B
Cornton (Down)	26A
Cornwall Jnc	3C
CORNWOOD	3C
CORPACH	31B
CORROUR	30B
CORSHAM	5C
CORWEN	15C
COSFORD HALT	10C
Cosford Siding	10C
COSHAM	5D
Cosham Jnc	5D
COTEHILL	13A
COTON HILL (GOODS)	10C
Coton Hill N Box	10C
Cottage Crossing (Down)	16A
COTTAM	6B
COTTINGHAM	20B
Cottingham Jnc	20B
COULSDON NORTH	7D
COULSDON SOUTH	7D
COUPAR ANGUS	26A
Court Sart Jnc	7C
Court Sart Jnc Box	8C
COVE BAY	27A, 26B
COVENTRY	4A
COWBIT	6B
Cowburn Tunnel	15A
Cowburn Tunnel West (Up)	15A
COWDENBEATH (NEW)	24B
Cowdenbeath Jnc	24B
Cowdenbeath N Jnc	24B
COWLAIRS	24B, 28B
Cowlairs E Jnc	28B
Cowlairs N Jnc	28B
Cowlairs W Jnc	28B
Cowley Bridge Jnc	2C, 2D
COWTON	3B
CRAIGELLACHIE	27B, 32B
CRAIGENDORAN	28B
Craigendoran Jnc	28B, 29B
Craigenhill (Up)	25A
Craiginches South (Up)	27A
CRAIGO	27A, 26B
CRAMLINGTON	3B
Cranham (Up)	18A
CRATHES	28B

CRAVEN ARMS & STOKESAY	2E
CRAWFORD	25A
CRAWLEY	9D
CRAYFORD	8D
Crayford Brick Siding Box	8D
Crayford Creek Jnc	8D
CREDITON	2D
Creech Jnc	2C, 6C
CREECH ST MICHAEL HALT	2C, 6C
CREEK MOOR HALT	1E
CREETOWN	30A
Cressbrook Tunnel	15A
CRESSINGTON	16B
CREWE	2A, 6A, 7A, 8A, 16C
CREWKERNE	2D
CREWS HILL	22B
CRIANLARICH	38A, 29B
Crianlarich Jnc	38A
CRICCIETH	15C
Crich Jnc (Up)	16A
Crick Tunnel	4A
CRICKLEWOOD	10A
Crigglestone (Down)	20A
Crigglestone Tunnel	20A
Crimple Jnc	8B
Crimple Tunnel	8B
CROFT	18A
CROFT SPA	3B
CROFTON PARK	12D
CROMDALE	32B
CROMER	10B
Cromer Jnc	10B
CROMFORD	15A
CROOKSTON	31A
CROPREDY	9C
CROSBY GARRETT	13A
CROSS GATES	8B, 18B, 19B
Cross Gates Jnc	8B, 19B
CROSS LANE	9A
CROSSGATES	24B
CROSSMICHAEL	30A
CROSSMYLOOF	30A
CROSTON	23A
Crow Nest Jnc (Up)	19A
CROW PARK	2B
CROWDEN	14B
CROWHURST	13D
Crowhurst Jnc	8D

Crowhurst Jnc South	13D	Dalgetty Box	25B	Deeside Tunnel	15C
CROWTHORNE	13D	DALGUISE	32A	DEFFORD	17A
CROXALL (CLOSED)	16A	Dallam Branch Sdgs (Down)	2A, 7A	DEFIANCE PLATFORM (CLOSED)	3C
CROXDALE (CLOSED)	3B	DALMALLY	38A	Delaney's Sidings (Up)	12A
CROY	24B	DALMENY	24B	DELNY	35A
Cruckmeole Jnc	14C	Dalmeny North Jnc	24B	Denbigh Hall (Up)	1A
CRUDGINGTON	16C	DALMUIR	28B	DENBY DALE	23A
CRWS-Y-NANT	15C	Dalmuir Jnc	28B	DENHAM	15B, 9C
Cuddington Cutting Box	4D	DALNASPIDAL	33A	DENHAM GOLF CLUB HALT	9C
CUDWORTH	11A, 14A	Dalquharran (Down)	31A	DENHAM GOLF CLUB PLATFORM	15B
Cudworth Stn S Jnc (Up)	11A, 14A	Dalraddy (Up)	33A	DENMARK HILL	12D
CUFFLEY & COFFS OAK	22B	DALREOCH	28B	DENT	13A
CULGAITH	13A	DALRY	31A	Dent Head (Down)	13A
Culgaith Tunnel	13A	Dalry No 3 (Down)	31A	DENTON	8A
CULHAM	11C	DALRY ROAD	32A	DENTON HALT	8D
CULLEN	27B	DALRYMPLE	31A	Denton Jnc (Up)	8A
CULLODEN MOOR	33A	Dalrymple Jnc (Up)	31A	DEPTFORD	8D
CULLOMPTON	2C	DALWHINNIE	33A	DERBY	15A, 16A
CULRAIN	35A	DANBY WISKE	3B	Derby N Jnc (Up)	15A
CULTER	28B	DANDALEITH	27B	Derby S Jnc (Up)	15A
CULTS	28B	Danesmoor Sidings (Down)	11A	Derrycombe Viaduct	3C
CULWORTH	13B	DANZEY	12C	Desborough N (Down)	10A
Culworth Jnc	13B, 15B	DARESBURY	7A	DESS	28B
CUMBERLAND ST	31A	DARFIELD	11A	DEVONPORT	3C, 3D
CUMBERNAULD	26A	DARLASTON	7A	Devonport Jnc	3C, 3D
Cumberworth Tunnel	23A	DARLEY DALE	15A	Devonshire Tunnel	1E
CUMMERTREES	29A	DARLINGTON	3B	DICCONSON LANE HALT	21A
CUMWHINTON	14A	DARNALL	14B	DIDCOT	5C, 11C
CUPAR	25B	Darnick Siding	21B	Didcot East Jnc	5C
CURRIEHILL	28A	DARSHAM	10B	Didcot N Jnc	11C
Curry Rivell Jnc	2C	DARTFORD	8D	Didcot W Curve Jnc	11C
Cuxton Rd Box	11D	Dartford Jnc	8D	DIDSBURY	15A
CYNWYD	15C	DARWEN	21A	DIGBY	6B
DAGENHAM	18A	DAUNTSEY	5C	DIGGLE	9A
DAILLY	31A	DAVA	34A	Diggle Jnc (Down)	9A
DAILUAINE HALT	32B	DAVIOT	33A	Diggle Water Troughs	9A
Dainton Siding	2C	DAWLISH	2C	Dillicar Troughs	3A
DAIRSIE	25B	DAWLISH WARREN	2C	DILTON MARSH HALT	14C
Dairy Jnc (Down)	32A	Dawsholm Bch Jnc	28B	Dingle Tunnel	16B
Dairy Jnc (Up)	28A	DEAL	11D	DINGWALL	35A, 36A
Dairy Middle Jnc (Down)	32A	Deal Jnc	12D	DINMORE	2E
DAISY HILL	19A	DEAN	5D	DINNET	28B
DAISYFIELD	21A	Dearne Jnc	15B	DINTING	14B
Daisyfield Jnc (Down)	21A, 23A	Dedham Box	9B	Dinting Viaduct	14B
Dalaraoch (Up)	32A	Dee Viaduct	10C	DINTON	1D
DALBEATTIE	30A	DEEPCAR	14B	DINWOODIE	24A
DALCROSS	34A	DEEPDENE	13D	Disley (Down)	15A
Dale Lane No 1 (Down)	19A	DEEPFIELDS	5A	Disley Tunnel	15A

DISS	9B	DRUMMUIR	27B	Dynevor Jnc North	8C
DITTON JNC	7A	Drump Lane Box	3C	DYSART	25B
Dobbs Brow Jnc (Down)	19A, 21A	Drumvaich Crossing	38A	E London Jnc	9B, 11B
Dock Jnc	7B	Dryclough Jnc (Up)	20A	E Suffolk Jnc	10B
DOCKYARD HALT	3C	DUBTON	27A	EAGLESCLIFFE	17B
DOE HILL	11A	Duckmanton S Jnc	14B	EALING BROADWAY	1C, 9C
DOLEHAM HALT	9D	DUDLEY PORT	5A	Earle's Sidings (Down)	15A
DOLGELLEY	15C	DUFFIELD	15A	EARLESTOWN JNC	7A, 9A
Dolphin Box	1C	DUFFTOWN	27B	EARLEY	13D
Dolphinton Jnc (Up)	28A	DUIRINISH	37A	EARLSFIELD	1D
DONCASTER	2B, 7B, 8B, 20B, 22B	DUKERIES JNC	2B	EARLSWOOD	7D
DONINGTON ROAD	6B	DUKINFIELD & ASHTON	8A	EARLSWOOD LAKES	12C
Doon Viaduct	31A	DULLATUR	24B	EASINGTON	17B
DORCHESTER	4C, 4D	DULLINGHAM	7B	EASSIE	26A
Dorchester Jnc	4C, 4D	DUMBARTON	28B	EAST BOLDON	17B
DORE & TOTLEY	14A, 15A	Dumbarton E Jnc	28B	EAST CROYDON	7D
Dore S Jnc (Down)	14A	DUMFRIES	29A, 30A	EAST DIDSBURY	8A
Dore W Jnc (Down)	15A	Dumfries No 4 (Up)	29A	EAST DULWICH	6D
DORKING NORTH	6D	DUMPTON PARK	11D	EAST FORTUNE	4B
DORKING TOWN	13D	DUNBALL	6C	East Gate Jnc	12B
DORMANS	8D	DUNBAR	4B	EAST GRINSTEAD (LOW LEVEL)	8D
DORTON HALT	9C	DUNBLANE	26A, 38A	EAST HAM	18A
DOUBLEBOIS	3C	DUNBRIDGE	5D	EAST HAVEN	26B
Douglas Bank (Up)	20A	DUNDEE (TAY BRIDGE)	25B	EAST HORNDON	18A
Douglas Park (Up)	25A	DUNDEE WEST	27A	EAST LANGTON	10A
DOUNE	38A	DUNFERMLINE (LOWER)	24B	EAST LEAKE	14B
Dove Holes (Down)	15A	DUNFORD BRIDGE	14B	EAST LINTON	4B
Dove Holes Tunnel	15A	DUNHAM HILL	7A	EAST MALLING HALT	12D
Dover Bridge (Down)	19A	Dunhampstead (Down)	17A	East Sutton Jnc	9B
DOVER MARINE	10D, 12D	DUNKELD	32A	EAST VILLE	5B
DOVER PRIORY	12D	DUNLOP	29A	EASTBOURNE	7D
DOVERCOURT BAY	12B	DUNNING	26A	EASTLEIGH	4D, 5D
DOVEY JNC	13C	Dunottar (Down)	27A	Eastleigh South Jnc	5D
DOWNFIELD CROSSING HALT	6C	DUNPHAIL	34A	EASTRIGGS	29A
Dr Day's Bridge Jnc	12C	DUNRAGIT	30A, 31A	EASTWOOD	19A
Drawbridge & Jnc	8C	DUNROBIN (PRIVATE)	35A	Eaton Crossing Box	12B
DRAYCOTT	15A	Dunrod (Down)	28A	EBBSFLEET & CLIFFSEND HALT	
DRAYTON GREEN HALT	9C	DUNSTALL PARK	10C	(CLOSED)	11D
DREM	4B	Dunton East (Down)	18A	Ebbw Jnc	7C
DRIFFIELD	18B	DUNTON GREEN	10D	EBLEY CROSSING HALT	6C
Droitwich Road (Down)	17A	Dunton West (Up)	18A	ECCLEFECHAN	24A
DRONFIELD	14A	DURHAM	3B	ECCLES	9A
DROYLSDEN	9A	Durran Hill South Sidings (Down)	14A	ECCLES ROAD	12B
Druimuachdar Summit	33A	DURRINGTON-BY-SEA	6D	Eccles Water Troughs	9A
DRUM	28B	DURSTON	6C	ECCLESFIELD	14A
DRUMCHAPEL	28B	Dutchlands Box	13B	ECKINGTON	17A, 14B
Drumlanrig Tunnel	29A	DYCE	26B, 32B	ECKINGTON & RENISHAW	11A
DRUMLITHIE	27A, 26B	DYFFRYN-ON-SEA	15C	EDALE	15A

EDDERTON	35A	Engine Shed Sidings Jnc	17A, 12C	FALLS OF CRUACHAN	38A
Eden Valley Jc (Up)	3A	Enham Box	1D	FALLSIDE	25A
EDENBRIDGE	13D	ENTHORPE	18B	FALMER	9D
Edendon (Down)	32A	ENTWISTLE	21A	FANGCROSS	20B
EDGE HILL	7A, 9A	EPSOM	4D, 6D	FAREHAM	5D, 9D
Edge Hill No 3 (Up)	7A	Epsom Common Box	6D	FARINGTON	3A, 22A
Edgeley No 1 (Down)	8A	ERITH	8D	Farington Curve Jnc (Down)	3A, 22A
EDINBURGH (PRINCES ST)	28A, 32A	ERROL	27A	Farington Curve Jnc (Up)	23A
EDINBURGH (WAVERLEY)	4B, 21B, 24B	Eryholme Jnc	3B	FARLINGTON HALT	5D
EDINGTON & BRATTON	1C	ESCRICK	2B	Farlington Jnc	5D
EDINGTON JNC	1E	ESHER	1D	FARNBOROUGH	1D
EDWALTON (CLOSED)	14A	ESKBANK	21B	FARNBOROUGH NORTH	13D
EGGESFORD	3D	ESPLANADE	25B	FARNCOMBE	5D
Egleton (Up)	14A	ESSENDINE	1B	FARNELL ROAD	27A
EGLINTON ST	25A	ESSLEMONT	32B	FARNINGHAM ROAD	11D
ELDERSLIE	31A	ETCHINGHAM	13D	FARNWORTH	22A, 16B
Elderslie No 1 (Up)	31A	ETRURIA	8A	Farnworth Tunnel	22A
Elderslie No 2 (Up)	30A, 31A	Etteridge (Up)	33A	FASLANE JNC	29B
Eldroth (Up)	18A	ETTINGSHALL ROAD	5A	FAULDHOUSE	28A
ELEPHANT & CASTLE	12D	EUSTON	1A	FAVERSHAM	11D, 12D
ELFORD	16A	Euxton Jnc (Down)	3A, 22A	Faversham Jnc	11D, 12D
ELGIN	34A, 27B	Euxton No 1 (Down)	22A	FAWKHAM	11D
ELLAND	19A	EVANTON	35A	Fawkham Jnc	11D
Elland Tunnel	19A	EVERCREECH (NEW)	1E	FAY GATE	9D
ELLESEMERE	13C	EVERCREECH JNC	1E	FAZAKERLEY	19A
ELLIOT JNC	26B	Evercreech Jnc North (Up)	1E	Fazakerley Jnc (Down)	19A
ELLON	32B	EVERINGHAM	18B	FEARN	35A
Elm Bridge (Up)	17A	EVERSHOT	4C	FELIN FRAN (GOODS)	8C
Elm Bridge Box	12C	EVESHAM	11C	FELIN FRAN HALT	8C
ELM PARK	18A	EWELL EAST	6D	Felin Fran West Jnc	8C
ELMESTHORPE	18A	EWELL WEST	4D	FELLING	17B
Elmhurst (Up)	2A	EXETER (ST DAVID'S)	2C, 2D	FENCHURCH ST	18A
ELMSTEAD WOODS	10D	EXETER CENTRAL	2D	FENNS BANK	13C
ELMSWELL	7B	EXMINSTER	2C	FENNY COMPTON	9C
ELSECAR	14A	Exmouth Jnc	2D	FERRIBY	18B
ELSENHAM	11B	EYDON ROAD HALT	15B	FERRYBRIDGE	15B, 19B
Elstow (Up)	10A	EYNSFORD	12D	FERRYHILL	3B
ELSTREE	10A	Eynsford Tunnel	12D	Ferryhill Jnc	26B, 28B
ELSWICK	22B	FAIRFIELD	16B	Ferryhill Jnc (Down)	27A
ELVANFOOT	25A	Fairfield Jnc	16B	FERRYSIDE	8C
ELY	6B, 7B, 11B, 7C	Fairfield Jnc	16B	FILTON JNC	12C
Ely N Jnc	11B	Fairwood Box	1C	Finchley Road (Down)	10A
Ely N Jnc	6B, 11B	Fairwood Jnc	1C	FINDOCHTY	27B
EMSWORTH	6D	Falahill Box	21B	FINEDON (Closed)	10A
Enborne Jnc	1C	FALKIRK (HIGH)	24B	FINMERE	13B
ENFIELD CHASE	22B	FALKLAND ROAD	25B	FINNINGHAM	9B
ENFIELD LOCK	11B	FALLODEN (PRIVATE)	4B	FINNINGLEY	7B
Engine Shed Jnc (Up)	11A	FALLOWFIELD	16B	FINSBURY PARK	1B

FINSTOCK ROAD BRIDGE HALT	11C	FORRES	34A	GALASHIELS	21B
Firsby S Jnc	5B	FORRES	34A	GALGATE (CLOSED)	3A
FISHBOURNE HALT	6D	FORSINARD	36A	Gamston Box	2B
FISHERGATE HALT	6D	FORT MATILDA	28A	Gannow Jnc (Down)	23A
Fisherton Tunnel	1D, 5D	Fort Pitt Tunnel	11D	Gannow Jnc (Up)	23A
FISHGUARD & GOODWICK	8C	FORT WILLIAM	30B	GANTON	19B
FISHGUARD HARBOUR	8C	FORTEVIOT	26A	GARELOCHHEAD	29B
FISKERTON	16A	FORTH BRIDGE	24B	GARFORTH	18B, 19B
FITZWILLIAM	8B	FORTHERBY	5B	GARGRAVE	12A
FLADBURY	11C	Foryd Jnc (Down)	6A	GARMOUTH	27B
FLAG STATION	15C	Fosse Road Box	9C	GARNKIRK	27A
FLAMBOROUGH	20B	FOULIS	35A	GARNOCK (EAST)	31A
FLAX BOURTON	5C	FOUNTAINHALL	21B	Garnqueen S Jnc (Down)	26A
Flax Bourton Cutting Box	5C	FOUR ASHES	5A	Garrochburn (Up)	29A
FLAXTON	19B	FOUR CROSSES	13C	GARSDALE	13A
FLEET	1D	FOURSTONES	22B	Garsdale Troughs	13A
FLEETWOOD	22A	Foxhall Jnc	5C	GARSTANG & CATTERALL	3A
FLEMINGTON	25A	Foxlow Jnc (Up)	11A	GARSTON	16B
Fletton Jnc Box	1B	FOXTON	5B	GARTCOSH	27A
FLINT	6A	Frampton Crossing Box	6C	Gartcosh Jnc (Up)	27A
Flint Water Troughs	6A	FRANKTON	13C	GARTSHERRIE (CLOSED)	26A
FLITWICK	10A	FRANT	13D	Gartsherrie L.N.E. Jnc (Up)	26A
FLIXTON	16B	FRASERBURGH	32B	GARVE	36A
FLORDON	10B	FRATTON	5D	Gas Factory Jnc (Down)	18A
FLORISTON	24A	FRENCH DROVE	6B	Gas Works Tunnel	1B
Fodderty Jnc	36A	FRESHFIELD	20A	GATEHOUSE OF FLEET	30A
FOGGATHORPE	18B	FRESHFORD	14C	GATESHEAD	17B
FOLKESTONE CENTRAL	10D	Friarton (Up)	26A	GATHURST	20A
FOLKESTONE HARBOUR	10D	FRIARY	3D	GATLEY	8A
FOLKESTONE JNC	10D	Friary Jnc	3D	GATWICK AIRPORT	7D
FORD	3D	FRICKLEY	15B	GATWICK RACECOURSE	7D
FORD BRIDGE	2E	FRITWELL & SOMERTON	11C	GEDDINGTON	14A
FORD HALT	3C	FROCESTER	17A, 12C	GEORGEMAS	36A, 38A
FORD HOUSES	5A	FRODSHAM	7A	GEORGETOWN	28A
FORDEN	13C	Frodsham Jnc	7A	Germiston Jnc (Up)	27A
Forder Viaduct	3C	Frodsham Tunnel	7A	GERRARDS CROSS	15B, 9C
Fordgate Box	6C	FROME	2C	GIDEA PARK	9B
FORDHAM	7B	Fryston South	19A	GIGGLESWICK	18A
FORDOUN	27A, 26B	FULBOURNE	7B	GILLETTS CROSSING HALT	22A
FOREGATE STREET	16C	Fullwood Jnc (Up)	27A, 28A	GILLINGHAM	2D, 11D
FOREST GATE	9B	Furnace Tunnel	20A	Gillingham Tunnel	2D
FOREST HALL	3B	FUSHIEBRIDGE (CLOSED)	21B	GILSLAND	22B
FOREST HILL	7D	Gaer Jnc	7C	GIRVAN	31A
FORFAR	26A	GAERWEN	6A	Girvan No 1 (Down)	31A
Forfar S Jnc (Down)	26A	GAILES	31A	GISBURN	21A
FORGANDENNY	26A	GAILEY	5A	GLAMIS	26A
FORMBY	20A	GAINSBOROUGH (CENTRAL)	23B	GLANDYFI	13C
FORNCETT	10B	GAINSBOROUGH (LEA ROAD)	7B	GLASGOW (ST ENOCH)	31A

GLASGOW (BUCHANAN ST)	27A	GOODRINGTON SANDS HALT	4C	Great Rocks Jnc (Down)	15A
GLASGOW (CENTRAL)	25A, 28A	GOOLE	20B	GREATHAM	17B
GLASGOW (QUEEN ST)	24B, 28B	Goole Swing Bridge	20B	Greenend Siding	21B
GLASGOW (STENOCH)	30A	Goose Hill Jnc (Up)	11A, 19A	GREENFIELD	9A
GLASSAUGH	27B	GOOSTREY	8A	GREENFORD	9C
GLASSEL	28B	GORDON HILL	22B	GREENHEAD	22B
GLASTERLAW	27A	GOREBRIDGE	21B	GREENHILL	26A
Glaston Tunnel	14A	GORING & STREATLEY	5C	Greenhill Upper Jnc	24B
GLASTONBURY & STREET	1E	GORING-BY-SEA	6D	GREENHITHE	8D
GLAZEBROOK	16B	GORTON	16B	GREENLOANING	26A
Glazebrook East Jnc	16B	GOSBERTON	6B	GREENOCK (CENTRAL)	28A
GLAZEBURY	9A	GOSWICK	4B	GREENOCK (LYNEDOCH)	30A
Glen Douglas	29B	Gothan Jnc	14B	GREENOCK (PRINCES PIER)	30A
GLENBARRY	27B	GOTHERINGTON	12C	GREENOCK (WEST)	28A
GLENBOIG	26A, 27A	GOUROCK	28A	GREENWICH	8D
GLENCARRON PLATFORM	36A	GOWERTON	8C	Greet Tunnel	12C
GLENCARSE	27A	GR MISSENDEN	13B	GREETLAND	19A
Glencruitten Crossing	38A	Grafton Curve Jnc	1C	Greetwell Jnc	6B
GLENDON & RUSHTON	10A	GRAHAMSTON	32A	Gregson Lane (Down)	23A
Glendon S Jnc	10A, 14A	GRAMPOUND ROAD	3C	Grendon Underwood Jnc	13B, 15B
GLENEAGLES	26A	Grand Jnc (Down)	5A	GRESFORD	10C
Glenesk Jnc	21B	Grand Jnc (Up)	17A	Greskine (Down)	24A
GLENFARG	24B	Grane Road Siding (Up)	23A	Gresty Lane No 2 (Down)	7A
GLENFINNAN	31B	GRANGE	27B	GRETNA	24A
GLENGARNOCK	31A	GRANGE COURT	6C	GRETNA GREEN	29A
Glenlochy Crossing	38A	Grange North Jnc	27B	Gretna Jnc (Up)	24A, 29A
Glenlochy Siding	30B	GRANGE PARK	22B	GRETTON	14A
GLENLUCE	30A	Grange Park Jnc	22B	GRETTON HALT	12C
Glenoglehead Crossing	38A	GRANGESTON HALT	31A	GRIMES HILL & WYTHAL	
GLENWHILLY	31A	GRANTHAM	2B	PLATFORM	12C
GLOUCESTER	17A, 6C	GRANTOWN-ON-SPEY	34A, 32B	Grimesthorpe No 1 (Up)	14A
Gloucester S Jnc	6C, 12C	GRANTSHOUSE	4B	GRIMSBY DOCKS	23B
GLYNDE	7D, 9D	Grasmoor Jnc	6B	GRIMSBY TOWN	5B
GLYNYFRDWY	15C	GRATELEY	1D	GRIMSTON	14A
GOBOWEN	10C	Graveney Box	11D	GRIMSTON & FRAMPTON	4C
Gobowen Jnc	10C, 13C	GRAVESEND CENTRAL	8D	Grimston Tunnel	14A
GODALMING	5D	GRAY RIGG	3A	GRINDLEFORD	15A
GODLEY JNC	14B	GREAT BARR	7A	Griseburn (Up)	13A
Godley Jnc	16B	GREAT BENTLEY	12B	GRISTHORPE	20B
Godscroft (Up)	7A	Great Bowden (Down)	10A	Grove Jnc	13D
GODSTONE	13D	GREAT BRIDGEFORD	2A	GROVE PARK	10D
GOGAR (CLOSED)	32A	GREAT COATES	23B	Grove Tunnel	13D
GOLBORNE	2A	Great George St Tunnel	16B	GT CHESTERFORD	11B
Golborne Jnc (Down)	2A	GREAT GLEN	10A	GUAY	32A
GOLLANFIELD JNC	34A	Great Harwood Jnc (Down)	23A	GUIDE BRIDGE	14B, 16B
GOLSPIE	35A	GREAT HAYWOOD	8A	Guilden Sutton Box (Up)	7A
GOMSHALL	13D	GREAT LONGSTONE	15A	GUILDFORD	5D, 13D
GOODMAYES	9B	GREAT PONTON	2B	Gumley (Down)	10A

HEATHWAY	18A	HEXHAM	22B	HIXON	8A
HEATON	3B	Hexthorpe Jnc	22B	HOCKLEY	12B, 10C
HEATON CHAPEL	8A	HEYFORD	11C	HODNET	16C
Heaton Lodge Jnc (Down)	19A	Heyford (Up)	1A	HOGHTON	23A
HEATON MERSEY	15A	HEYSHAM HARBOUR	18A	HOLBECK	20A
Heaton Mersey East Jnc (Up)	16B	Heysham Harbour Jnc (Down)	18A	HOLBECK (HIGH LEVEL)	8B
HEATON NORRIS	8A	Heysham Moss Sidings (Down)	18A	HOLBECK (LOW LEVEL)	11A, 8B
Heaton Norris No 2 (Up)	8A	HEYTESBURY	14C	HOLBORN VIADUCT	12D
HEBDEN BRIDGE	19A	Heywood Road Jnc	1C	Holbrook Park Troughs	4A
HECK	2B	Hickleton Main Colliery Sidings		Holes Bay Jnc	4D, 1E
HECKMONDWIKE	20A	(Down)	15B	Holland Moss Siding	19A
Heddon Mill Crossing	3D	HIGH BROOMS	13D	HOLLAND ROAD HALT	6D
HEELEY	14A	High Peak Jnc (Up)	15A	HOLLINGBOURNE	12D
HELE & BRADNINCH	2C	High St (Down)	17A	Hollinswood (Goods)	10C
HELENSBURGH	28B	High Tor Tunnels	15A	HOLME	23A, 1B
HELENSBURGH (UPPER)	29B	HIGH WYCOMBE	15B, 9C	HOLME MOORE	18B
HELLIFIELD	12A, 21A	HIGHAM	7B, 8D	HOLMES	14A
Helm Tunnel	13A	HIGHBRIDGE	6C, 1E	HOLMES CHAPEL	8A
HELMDON	13B	HIGHFIELD	18B	HOLMSLEY	3D
HELMSDALE	36A	HIGHTOWN	20A	HOLMWOOD	6D
HELMSHORE	23A	Highworth Jnc	5C	HOLT JNC	4C
HELPRINGHAM	6B	HILDENBOROUGH	10D	HOLTON HEATH	4D
Helpston Box	1B	Hill House Box	9B	HOLTON VILLAGE	5B
HELSBY	7A	Hillfield Tunnel	7C	HOLTON-LE-CLAY	5B
Helwith Bridge (Up)	12A	Hillhouse No 2 Jnc (Up)	23A	Holwell Sidings (Down)	14A
HEMEL HEMPSTEAD	1A	HILLINGTON	28A, 31A	HOLYHEAD	7A
Hemerdon Siding	3C	HILLINGTON (EAST)	28A, 31A	HOLYTOWN	27A, 28A
HEMINGBROUGH	18B	Hillmorton (Down)	4A	Holytown Jnc (Down)	27A, 28A
HEMSWORTH	8B	HILLSIDE	20A, 26B	HOLYWELL JNC	6A
HENDON	10A	HILLSIDE	26B	HOLYWOOD	29A
HENFIELD	8D	Hilmorton (Up)	1A	HONEYBOURNE	11C
HENLEY-IN-ARDEN	12C	HILSEA HALT	5D	Honeybourne E Jnc	12C
HENSTRIDGE	1E	HILTON HOUSE	21A	Honeybourne S Jnc	11C
HENWICK	16C	Hilton Jnc	24B	Honeybourne W Jnc	12C
HEREFORD (BARRS COURT)	2E	Hilton Jnc (Up)	26A	HONITON	2D
HERIOT	21B	Hincaster Jc (Down)	3A	Honiton Incline Box	2D
HERNE BAY	11D	HINCKLEY	18A	Honiton Tunnel	2D
HERNE HILL	11D, 12D	HINDLEY	19A	HONLEY	23A
Herringe Box	10D	Hindley & Blackrod Branch Jnc		HONOR OAK PARK	7D
HERSHAM	1D	(Down)	21A	Hoo Jnc	8D
HERTFORD NORTH	22B	Hindley No 2 Jnc (Down)	19A	HOOK	1D
HESLERTON	19B	Hindley No 3 (Up)	19A	HOPE	15A
HESSLE	18B	Hindley No 3 Jnc (Down)	20A	HORBURY (MILLFIELD ROAD)	19A
Hessle Road Jnc	18B	HINTON ADMIRAL	4D	HORBURY & OSSETT	19A
HEST BANK	3A	HIPPERHOLME	20A	HORDEN	17B
Hest Bank Troughs	3A	HITCHIN	1B, 5B	HORFIELD PLATFORM	12C
HETHERSETT	12B	HITHER GREEN	8D, 10D	HORLEY	7D
Hewish Crossing Box	2D	Hither Green Jnc	8D	HORNBY	18A

HORNCHURCH	18A	IBROX	28A, 31A	KEGWORTH	11A
HORNSEY	1B	IDMISTON HALT	1D	KEIGHLEY	12A
HORSFORTH	8B	Idsworth Crossing	5D	KEINTON MANDEVILLE	2C
HORSHAM	6D, 9D	IFIELD	9D	KEITH	34A, 27B
HORSTED KEYNES	8D	ILFORD	9B	KEITH TOWN	27B
HORTON-IN-RIBBLESDALE	12A	ILFRACOMBE	3D	KELSTON	17A
Horwich Fork Jnc (Down)	21A, 22A	ILKESTON JNC	11A	KELVEDON	9B
HOSCAR	20A	ILMER HALT	15B, 9C	KEMBLE	6C
HOTHFIELD HALT	12D	INCE	20A	Kempston Rd Jnc (Up)	10A
HOUGH GREEN	16B	Inchcoonans (Up)	27A	KEMSING	12D
HOUGHAM	2B	Inchlea Crossing (Up)	33A	Ken Viaduct	30A
Houghton Colliery Sidings	11A	Inchmagranachan Crossing Loop (Up)	32A	KENNETHMONT	27B
Houghton Conquest (Up)	10A	INCHTURE	27A	KENNETT	7B
HOUSTON & CROSSLEE	30A	INGATESTONE	9B	Kennington Jnc	11C
HOVE	6D	Ingrave Box	9B	KENNISHEAD	30A
HOW MILL	22B	INNERWICK	4B	KENSAL GREEN	1A
Howes Siding (Down)	14A	INSCH	26B	KENT HOUSE	11D
Howsham Gates	19B	Inver Tunnel	32A	KENTISH TOWN	10A
HOWWOOD	31A	INVERAMSAY	26B	KENTON	1A
HOY	38A	INVERESK	4B	KENYON JNC	9A
HUCKNALL CENTRAL	14B	INVERGORDON	35A	KERSHOPE FOOT	21B
HUDDERSFIELD	23A	INVERGOWRIE	27A	Ketley Jnc	10C
HULL	18B, 20B	INVERKEILOR	26B	KETTERING	10A, 14A
HULLAVINGTON	7C	INVERKEITHING	24B	Kettering Iron & Coal Co (Up)	10A
Humber Road Jnc (Up)	4A	INVERKIP	28A	Kettering Iron & Coal Co Sidings	
HUMBERSTONE ROAD	10A	INVERNESS	33A, 34A, 35A	(Down)	14A
HUNCOAT	23A	INVERSHIN	35A	Kettering Jnc (Up)	10A
Huncoat Brick Siding (Down)	23A	INVERUGIE	32B	Ketteringham Box	12B
HUNGERFORD	1C	INVERUGLAS	29B	Kettleby Crossing	23B
HUNMANBY	20B	INVERURIE	26B	KEYHAM	3C
Hunsbury Hill Tunnel	4A	IPSWICH	9B, 10B	Keymer Jnc	7D
HUNSLET	11A	IRCHESTER	10A	KEYNSHAM	5C
Hunting Butts Tunnel	12C	Irchester Jnc (Up)	10A	KIBWORTH	10A
HUNTINGDON	1B	IRLAM	16B	Kibworth N (Down)	10A
HUNTLY	27B	Ironhirst (Up)	29A	KIDLINGTON	11C
HUNTS CROSS	16B	IRVINE	31A	KIDSGROVE (CENTRAL)	8A
Hunts Cross West Jnc (Down)	16B	Itchingfield Jnc	6D, 8D	KIDWELLY	8C
HURLFORD	29A	IVER	1C	KIDWELLY PLATS HALT	8C
HURST GREEN HALT	8D	IVYBRIDGE	3C	KILBARCHAN	31A
Hurst Green Jnc	8D	Jersey Marine Jnc North	8C	KILBIRNIE	31A
HURSTBOURNE	1D	JOHNSTONE	31A	Kilbowie (Old St) Jnc	28B
HUTTONS AMBO	19B	JOHNSTONE NORTH	31A	KILBURN HIGH ROAD	1A
HUYTON	9A	JOHNSTOWN & HAFOD	10C	Kilby Bridge (Down)	10A
HUYTON QUARRY	9A	JOPPA	4B	KILDARY	35A
Hyde Jnc	14B	JORDANSTON HALT	8C	KILDONAN	36A
HYDE ROAD	16B	Junc New Holland Branch	23B	KILDWICK & CROSSHILLS	12A
HYKEHAM	16A	KEARSLEY	22A	KILKERRAN	31A
HYTHE	12B	KEARSNEY	12D	KILLAMARSH	11A, 14B

KILLIECRANKIE	32A	KINTBURY	1C	LAKENHEATH	11B
Killiecrankie Tunnel	32A	KINTORE	26B	Laleston Box	7C
KILLIN JNC	38A	KIPLING COTES	20B	Lambrigg Crossing (Up)	3A
KILLINGWORTH	3B	KIRKBY	19A	LAMINGTON	25A
KILLOCHAN	31A	KIRKBY BENTWICK	14B	Lanark Jnc (Down)	25A
KILLYWHAN	30A	Kirkby South Jnc	14B	LANCASTER (CASTLE)	3A
KILMACOLM	30A	KIRKBY STEPHEN	13A	LANCASTER (GREEN AYRE)	18A
KILMARNOCK	29A	KIRKCALDY	25B	Lancaster No 1 (Down)	3A
Kilmarnock No 1 (Down)	29A	KIRKCONNEL	29A	LANCING	6D
KILMAURS	29A	KIRKCOWAN	30A	LANDO PLATFORM HALT	8C
KILNHURST	11A, 15B	KIRKDALE	19A	Landor St Jnc (Down)	17A
Kilnknowe Jnc	21B	KIRKGUNZEON	30A	Landor St Jnc (Up)	16A
KILPATRICK	28B	KIRKHAM & WESHAM	22A	LANDORE (HIGH LEVEL)	8C
KILSBY & CRICK	4A	KIRKHAM ABBEY	19B	Landore Viaduct	8C
Kilsby Tunnel	1A	Kirkham N Jnc (Down)	22A	LANGBANK	28A
Kilsby Tunnel N (Down)	1A	Kirkham N Jnc (Up)	22A	LANGFORD (GOODS)	14C
KILWINNING	31A	KIRKPATRICK	24A	Langham Jnc (Down)	14A
Kimbridge Jnc	5D	KIRKSTALL	11A	LANGHO	21A
KINALDIE	26B	Kirriemuir Jnc (Up)	26A	LANGLEY	1C
KINBRACE	36A	KIRTLEBRIDGE	24A	Langley Jnc	1B, 22B
KINBUCK	26A	KIRTON	5B	LANGLEY MILL	11A
KINCRAIG	33A	Kirton Lane Sidings	23B	Langley Water Troughs	1B
KINFAUNS	27A	KIRTON LINDSEY	23B	LANGPORT EAST	2C
King Edward Bridge Jnc	3B	Kitsonwood Tunnel	23A	LANGWATHBY	13A
King William Siding	21A	KITTYBREWSTER	26B, 32B	Lansdown Jnc	12C
KING'S LANGLEY	1A	KIVETON BRIDGE	16B	Lansdown Jnc (Down)	17A
KINGHAM	11C	KIVETON PARK	16B	LAPFORD	3D
KINGHORN	25B	KNAPTON	19B	LAPWORTH	9C
Kinghorn Tunnel	25B	KNEBWORTH	1B	LARBERT	26A, 32A
KINGKERSWELL	4C	Knight's Hill Tunnel	6D	Larbert Jnc	32A
Kingmoor (Down)	24A	Knighton Crossing	5C	Larbert Jnc (Down)	26A
KINGS HEATH (CLOSED)	16A	Knighton N Jnc (Down)	10A	Largin Box & Viaduct	3C
KINGS NORTON	16A, 17A	Knighton Tunnel	10A	LAURENCEKIRK	27A, 26B
KINGS SUTTON	9C	Knightswood N Jnc	28B	Laverstock Box	1D
KINGSBURY	16A	KNOCK	27B	LAVERTON HALT	12C
KINGSCOTE	8D	KNOCKANDE	32B	LAVINGTON	1C
KINGSHOUSE PLATFORM	38A	KNOCKHOLT	10D	LAW JNC	25A, 27A
KINGSKETTLE	25B	KNOTTINGLEY	19B	LAWRENCE HILL	12C
KINGSKNOWE	28A	KNOWLE & DORRIDGE	10C	Lawrence Hill Jnc (Down)	17A
KINGSWEAR	4C	Knowle Jnc	5D	LAYTON	21A
KINGSWEAR CROSSING HALT	4C	KYLE OF LOCHALSH	37A	LAZONBY	13A
Kingswood Crossing (Up)	32A	LACOCK HALT	4C	Lazonby Tunnel	13A
Kingswood Jnc (Down)	17A	LADYBANK	25B	LEA	7B
KINGUSSIE	33A	LAINDON	18A	LEA GREEN	9A
KINLOSS	34A	LAIRA HALT (CLOSED)	3C	LEA HALL	5A
Kinnaber Jnc	26B	Laira Jnc	3C	LEA ROAD (CLOSED)	22A
Kinnaber Jnc (Up)	27A	LAIRG	35A	Lea Wood Tunnel	15A
KINROSS JNC	24B	LAISTER DYKE	20A, 8B	LEAGRAVE	10A

LEAMINGTON SPA	9C	LISKEARD	3C	LLANTRISANT	7C
LEATHERHEAD	6D	LISS	5D	LLANVIHANGEL	2E
LEATON	10C	Litchfield Box	4D	LLANWERN	7C
LEDBURY	16C	Litchfield Tunnel	4D	Llanyfelach Tunnel	8C
LEE	8D	Litterbury	11B	LLANYMYNECH	13C
Lee Jnc	8D	LITTLE BYTHAM	1B	LLYNCLYS	13C
LEEBOTWOOD	2E	Little Eaton Jnc (Up)	15A	LLYSFAEN (Closed)	6A
LEEDS (CENTRAL)	20A, 8B	Little Fleet Viaduct	30A	LNER Level Crossing (Up)	16A
LEEDS (CITY)	8B, 18B, 19B	LITTLE MILL	4B	LOCH AWE	38A
Leeds Jnc (Down)	12A	Little Mill Jnc	2E	LOCH SKERROW PLATFORM	30A
LEGBOURNE ROAD	5B	LITTLE SALKELD	13A	LOCHANHEAD (CLOSED)	30A
Leggatfoot (Down)	25A	LITTLE SOMERFORD	7C	LOCHBURN (GOODS)	28B
LEICESTER	10A	LITTLE STEEPING	5B	LOCHEILSIDE	31B
LEICESTER (CENTRAL)	14B	LITTLE STRETTON HALT	2E	Lochgreen Jnc (Up)	31A
Leicester Goods Jnc South	14B	LITTLEBOROUGH	19A	LOCHLUICHART	36A
Leicester Jnc (Up)	16A	LITTLEHAVEN HALT	9D	Lochmuir Box	25B
LEIGH-ON-SEA	18A	LITTLETON & BADSEY	11C	LOCHSIDE	31A
Leigham Tunnel	6D	Littlewood Tile Siding (Up)	23A	LOCHWINNOCH	31A
LENHAM	12D	LITTLEWORTH	5B	LOCKAILORT	31B
Lenton N Jnc (Down)	14A	Litton Tunnel	15A	LOCKERBIE	24A
Lenton S Jnc (Down)	16A	LIVERPOOL (CENTRAL)	16B	Lockinge Box	5C
LENTRAN	35A	LIVERPOOL (EXCHANGE)	19A, 20A	LOCKWOOD	23A
LENZIE JNC	24B	LIVERPOOL (LIME ST)	7A, 9A	Lodge Farm Box (Closed)	6D
LEOMINSTER	2E	LIVERPOOL STREET	9B, 11B	LOFTHOUSE	8B
Leominster Jnc	16C	LIVERSEDGE	20A	LOGIERIEVE	32B
Lesmahagow Jnc (Up)	25A, 26A	LLANBEDR & PENSARN	15C	Lon Las Jnc	8C
LETCHWORTH	5B	LLANBRYNMAIR	13C	LONDESBOROUGH	20B
LETHAM GRANGE	26B	LLANDARCY HALT	8C	LONDON (KINGS CROSS)	1B
Letterston Jnc	8C	LLANDDERFEL	15C	LONDON BRIDGE	6D, 7D, 10D
LEUCHARS JNC	25B	Llandderfel Tunnel	15C	LONDON FIELDS	11B
LEVENSHULME	8A, 16B	Llandegai Tunnel	6A	LONDON ROAD	9D
LEVERTON	6B	Llandilo Jnc East	8C	London Road Jnc	15A
LEWES	7D, 9D	LLANDRE	13C	LONG ASHTON PLATFORM	5C
LEYLAND	3A, 22A	LLANDRILLO	15C	LONG BUCKBY	4A
Leys Box	1B	LLANDUDNO JNC	6A	LONG EATON	11A
LHANBRYDE	34A	LLANDULAS	6A	Long Eaton Jnc (Down)	16A
LICHFIELD (T.V. Low Level)	2A	LLANELLY	8C	LONG MARSTON	12C
LIFFORD (CLOSED)	16A	LLANFAIR	6A	LONG MARTON	13A
LIGHTCLIFFE	20A	LLANFEIRFECHAN	6A	LONG PRESTON	12A
LIMPLEY STOKE	14C	LLANGENNECH	8C	Long Rock Box	4C
LINCOLN	16A, 6B, 7B	LLANGFELACH (GOODS)	8C	LONG SUTTON & PITNEY	2C
LINGFIELD	8D	LLANGOLLEN	15C	Longfield Siding	11D
Lingfield Intermediate Box	8D	Llangollen Jnc	15C	LONGFORGAN	27A
LINLITHGOW	32A, 24B	Llangollen Line Jnc	10C	LONGHIRST	3B
LION'S HOLT HALT	2D	LLANHARAN	7C	LONGHOUGHTON	4B
LIPHOOK	5D	LLANSAMLET	8C	LONGMORN	27B
Lipson Jnc	3C, 3D	Llanstephan Crossing Box	8C	LONGNIDDRY	4B
LIPSON VALE HALT	3D	LLANTARNAM	2E	LONGPORT	8A

LONGSIDE	32B	LYGHE HALT	13D	MANTON	14A
LONGSIGHT	8A	Lymington Jnc	3D, 4D	Manton Tunnel	14A
LONGTOWN	21B	LYNDHURST	4D	Manton Wood Jnc (Down)	16B
LONMAY	32B	LYNESIDE (CLOSED)	21B	MANUEL	24B
Lords Tunnel	13B	Lynher Viaduct	3C	MARAZION	4C
LOSTOCK HALL	23A	LYTHAM	22A	MARCH	6B
Lostock Hall Jnc (Up)	23A	MACCLESFIELD	8A	March S Jnc	6B
LOSTOCK JNC	22A	Macclesfield Moss Box (Up)	8A	MARDEN	10D
Lostock Lane (Down)	22A	MACHYNLLETH	13C	Margam Moors Box	7C
LOSTWITHIEL	3C	MADELEY	2A	Margam Sidings West	7C
LOTH	35A	Madeley Jnc	10C	MARGATE	11D
LOUGHBOROUGH	11A	Madgescroft (Up)	26A	MARGATE EAST	11D
LOUGHBOROUGH (CENTRAL)	14B	MAGDALEN GREEN	27A	MARKET DRAYTON	16C
LOUGHBOROUGH JNC	12D	MAGHULL	23A	Market Drayton Jnc	7A, 10C, 16C
Loughborough Troughs	11A	MAGOR	7C	MARKET HARBOROUGH	10A
LOUGHOR	8C	MAIDEN NEWTON	4C	MARKET WEIGHTON	18B, 20B
Loughor Viaduct	8C	MAIDENHEAD	1C	Markham Box	2B
Loughton Siding (Down)	1A	MAIDSTONE EAST	12D	MARKINCH	25B
LOUTH	5B	Maindee E Jnc	7C	MARKS TEY	9B
Low Bentham (Down)	18A	Maindee N Jnc	2E	Marley Green Crossing	7A
LOW FELL	3B	MALDEN	1D	Marley Jnc (Down)	12A
LOW GILL	3A	MALLAIG	31B	Marley Tunnel	3C
Low House Crossing (Up)	13A	Mallaig Jnc	30B, 31B	MARSH BROOK	2E
LOW MOOR	20A	Mallerstang (Up)	13A	Marsh Farm Jnc	2E
Low Moor No 5 Jnc (Down)	20A	MALLING	12D	MARSH LANE	8B, 18B, 19B
LOW ROW	22B	MALTON	19B	MARSH LANE & LITHERLAND	20A
LOWDHAM	16A	MALVERN (GREAT)	16C	Marshall Meadows Box	4B
LOWER DARWEN	21A	MALVERN LINK	16C	Marshall's Siding (Up)	20A
LOWER PONTNEWYDD	2E	Malvern Road Jnc	12C	MARSHFIELD	7C
LOWESTOFT CENTRAL	12B	MALVERN WELLS	16C	Marshland Jnc	20B
Lowfield Jnc	22B	MANCHESTER (CENTRAL)	15A, 16B	MARSTEN GREEN	5A
LOWTHORPE	18B	MANCHESTER (LONDON ROAD)		Marston Crossing	5C
LUCKER	4B		8A, 16B	MARSTON MAGNA	4C
Lucker Water Troughs	4B	MANCHESTER (VICTORIA)	9A, 19A	Martello Tunnel	10D
LUDBOROUGH	5B	MANCHESTER EXCHANGE	9A	MARTIN MILL	11D
LUDDENDENFOOT	19A	Manchester Ship Canal Bridge	16B	Marton (Up)	22A
LUDLOW	2E	MANEA	6B	MARYHILL	28B
LUGTON	30A	MANGOTSFIELD	17A	Maryhill Cent Jnc	28B
LUIB	38A	Mangotsfield N Jnc (Down)	17A	Maryhill E Jnc	28B
LULLINGSTONE	12D	Mangotsfield S Jnc (No Box)	17A	MARYKIRK	27A, 26B
LUMPHANAN	28B	MANNINGTREE	12B	MARYLAND	9B
LUNAN BAY	26B	MANNINGTREE NORTH JNC	9B	MARYLEBONE	13B
LUNCARTY	26A, 32A	MANOR PARK	9B	Masboro S Jnc	11A
LUTON	10A	Manorowen Box	8C	MASBURY HALT	1E
LUTTERWORTH	13B	MANORS EAST	3B	MATHRY ROAD	8C
Lydden Tunnel	12D	Mansfield Jnc (Down)	14A	MATLOCK	15A
LYDFORD	3D	Mansfield Jnc (Up)	16A	MATLOCK BATH	15A
LYDNEY	6C	Mansfield Road Tunnel	14B	MAUCHLINE	29A

MAUD	32B	MIDGE HALL	23A	MONK FRYSTON	15B, 19A, 19B
Maudland Viaduct (Down)	22A	MIDGHAM	1C	Monk Spring Jnc (Down)	14A
MAULDETH ROAD	8A	Midland Jnc (Down)	18A	MONKTON (CLOSED)	31A
MAWCARSE JNC	24B	MIDSOMER NORTON & WELTON	1E	MONKTON & CAME HALT	4C, 4D
MAXWELLTOWN(CLOSED)	30A	MILBORNE PORT	2D	Monktonhall Jnc Box	4B
MAYBOLE	31A	MILCOTE	12C	MONKWEARMOUTH	17B
Maybole (Down)	31A	MILES PLATTING	9A	Monmore Green (Down)	5A
MAZE HILL	8D	MILFORD	5D	MONSAL DALE	15A
Meldon Jnc	2D	MILFORD & BROCTON	2A	Monsall Lane (Up)	19A
Meldon Viaduct	2D	Milford Jnc	15B, 19B, 5D	MONTGOMERY	13C
MELDRETH	5B	MILFORD JNC (CLOSED)	19A	MONTROSE	26B
MELKSHAM	4C	Milford Tunnel	15A	MONUMENT LANE	5A
MELLIS	9B	MILL HILL	10A, 23A	MOOR PARK & SANDY LODGE	13B
MELMERBY	17B	Mill Lane Jnc	20A	Moorcock Tunnel	13A
MELROSE	21B	MILLBAY	3C	MOORE (CLOSED)	2A
MELTON	10B	MILLBROOK	4D, 9D	Moore Troughs	2A
Melton Jnc (Up)	14A	Millbrook (Down)	10A	Moorewood (up)	1E
MELTON MOWBRAY	14A	Millburn Jnc (Down)	33A, 34A	MOORGATE HALT	9A
Melton Ross	23B	MILLERHILL	21B	MOORSIDE	19A
Melton Troughs	14A	MILLERS DALE	15A	Moorswater Viaduct	3C
MENAI BRIDGE	6A	Millers Dale Jnc (Down)	15A	MOORTHORPE	15B
MENHENIOT	3C	MILLHOUSES	14A	Moorthorpe N Jnc	15B
MENTHORPE GATE	18B	MILLIKEN PARK	31A	MORAR	31B
MEOPHAM	11D	Mills Hill (Down)	19A	MORCHARD ROAD	3D
MERCHISTON	28A	Millwood Tunnel	19A	Morecambe South Jnc	3A
MERSEY ROAD	16B	MILNATHORT	24B	MORETON	4D
MERSTHAM	7D	Milner Royd Jnc (Down)	19A, 20A	Moreton Cutting Box	5C
Merstham Quarry Tunnel	7D	Milngavie Jnc	28B	MORETON-IN-MARSH	11C
Merstham Tunnel	7D	MILNTHORPE	3A	MORETON-ON-LUGG	2E
METHLEY	11A	Milnwood Jnc (Up)	26A	Morlais E Jnc	8C
Methley Jnc (Down)	11A	Milton Jnc (Up)	27A	Morlais S Jnc	8C
Mexboro W Jnc	15B	MILTON RANGE HALT	8D	MORMOND HALT	32B
MEXBOROUGH	22B	MINETY & ASHTON KEYNES	6C	MORPETH	3B
MICHELDEVER	4D	MINFFORDD	15C	Morriston Viaduct	8C
MICKLE TRAFFORD	7A	MINSHULL VERNON (CLOSED)	2A	MORTEHOE	3D
MICKLEFIELD	18B, 19B	Minster East Jnc	11D	MORTIMER	4C
Mickleham Tunnel	6D	MINTLAW	32B	Morton Sidings (Up)	11A
MICKLETON HALT (CLOSED)	11C	MIRFIELD	19A	Mosedale Hall Crossing (Down)	3A
Mickley Box	22B	Miskin Crossing	7C	MOSELEY (CLOSED)	16A
MIDCALDER	28A	MISTERTON	7B	MOSES GATE	22A
Midcalder Jnc (Down)	28A	MISTLEY	12B	MOSS	2B
Midcalder Jnc (Up)	28A	MITCHAM JNC	6D	Moss Lane Jnc (Down)	23A
Middle Hill Tunnel	5C	MOAT LINE JNC	13C	Moss Lane Jnc (Up)	23A
Middlestown Jnc (Down)	20A	MOCHDRE & PABO (Closed)	6A	MOSS SIDE	22A
Middleton (Up)	4A	Mold Jnc No 1 (Down)	6A	Mossband (Down)	24A
MIDDLETON JNC	19A	Molewood Tunnel	22B	MOSSEND	26A, 27A
MIDDLETON-ON-THE-WOLDS	18B	Moncrieff Tunnel	26A	Mossend No 4 (Down)	28A
MIDFORD	1E	MONFIETH	26B	Mossgiel Tunnel	29A

MOSSLEY	9A	NEEDHAM	9B	NEWSHOLME	21A
MOSSLEY HILL	7A	Neilsons Sidings (Up)	10A	NEWTON	14B, 25A
MOSSPARK (WEST)	31A	NEILSTON	30A	NEWTON ABBOT	2C, 4C
MOSSTOWIE	34A	NELSON	23A	NEWTON HEATH	19A
MOSTON	19A	NETHERCLEUGH	24A	NEWTON KYME	19B
MOSTYN	6A	NETHY BRIDGE	32B	NEWTON ROAD	7A
MOTHERWELL	25A	NETLEY	9D	NEWTON ST CYRES	2D
MOTSPUR PARK	4D	Neville Hill Jnc	18B, 19B	NEWTON STEWART	30A
MOTTINGHAM	8D	NEW BARNET	1B	NEWTON-LE-WILLOWS	9A
MOTTRAM	14B	NEW BASFORD	14B	NEWTON-ON-AYR	31A
Mottram Viaduct	14B	NEW BIGGIN	13A	NEWTONGRANGE	21B
Moulinearn Crossing (Up)	32A	NEW CROSS	10D	NEWTONHILL	26B, 27A
Mount Gould Jnc	3D	NEW CROSS GATE	7D	NEWTONMORE	33A
MOUNTFIELD HALT	13D	NEW CUMNOCK	29A	NEWTOWN	13C
Mountfield Tunnel	13D	NEW ELTHAM	8D	NEWTOWN (GOODS)	7C
Mountnessing Box	12B	New England North Jnc	1B	Newtown W Box	7C
MOW COP	8A	NEW GALLOWAY	30A	NIDD BRIDGE	17B
MOY	33A	NEW HADLEY HALT	10C	Niddrie S Jnc	21B
MUCHALLS	27A, 26B	NEW HAILES	4B	NIGG	35A
MUIR OF ORD	35A	New Hall Box	9B	Ninewells Jnc (Up)	27A
MULBEN	34A	NEW HALL BRIDGE HALT	23A	NITSHILL	30A
MURROW	6B	New Hucknall Sidings	14B	NOCTON	6B
Murthat (Closed – Down)	24A	NEW LANE	20A	NORBURY	7D
MURTHLY	32A	NEW LUCE	31A	Normans Bank (Up)	15A
Muskham Box	2B	New Mills S Jnc (Down)	15A	NORMANS BAY HALT	9D
Muskham Water Troughs	2B	NEW MILTON	4D	NORMANTON	11A, 19A
Muspratts Siding (Down)	6A	NEW SOUTHGATE	1B	NORTH CAMP	13D
MUTLEY	3D	NEWARK	16A, 2B	NORTH DULWICH	6D
MUTLEY (CLOSED)	3C	Newbold (Down)	1A	North End Sidings	8D
Mutley Tunnel	3C, 3D	NEWBURY	1C	NORTH HARROW	13B
Myrtle Hill Jnc	8C	NEWBURY RACE COURSE	1C	NORTH HOWDEN	18B
MYTHOLMROYD	19A	NEWCASTLE CENTRAL	3B, 17B, 22B	North Kent East Jnc	8D
Naas Crossing (Up)	17A	Newcastle Crossing (Up)	7A	NORTH QUEENSFERRY	24B
NABURN	2B	NEWCASTLETON	21B	NORTH ROAD	3C, 3D
NAFFERTON	18B	NEWHAM	4B	NORTH RODE	8A
NAILSEA & BACKWELL	5C	NEWHAVEN HARBOUR	7D	North Rode Jnc (Up)	8A
NAIRN	34A	NEWHAVEN TOWN	7D	North Rode Viaduct	8A
Nant Hall (Down)	6A	NEWLAY & HORSFORTH	11A	North Somerset Jnc	5C
NANTWICH	7A, 16C	NEWMACHAR	32B	North Stoke Tunnel	6D
NANTYDERRY	2E	NEWMARKET	7B	NORTH TAWTON	2D
NAPSBURY	10A	Newmarket Yard Jnc	7B	NORTH THORSEBY	5B
NARBOROUGH	18A	Newmill Siding	26B	NORTH WALSHAM	10B
NAWORTH	22B	NEWNHAM	6C	NORTH WEMBLEY	1A
Neasden S Jnc	13B, 15B	Newnham Siding	1D	NORTHALLERTON	3B, 17B
NEATH (GENERAL)	7C	NEWPARK	28A	Northallerton Low Jnc	17B
Neath Engine Shed Box	7C	NEWPORT	7C, 2E	Northam Jnc	4D, 9D
Neath Jnc	8C	NEWPORT (ESSEX)	11B	NORTHAMPTON (CASTLE)	4A
Neath River Swing Bridge	8C	NEWSEAT HALT	32B	Northchurch (Down)	1A

Northchurch Tunnel	1A	OFFORD	1B	Oxheys (Down)	3A
NORTHENDEN	16B	OKEHAMPTON	2D	Oxley North Jnc	10C
NORTHFIELD	16A	OLD COLWYN	6A	OXTED	8D
NORTHFLEET	8D	OLD CUMNOCK	29A	Oxted Lime Sidings Box	8D
NORTHOLT	9C	OLD DALBY	14A	Oxwell Mains Siding	4B
NORTHOLT PARK	15B	Old Distillery Siding	30B	OYNE	26B
NORTHORPE	23B	OLD LEAKE	5B	PADDINGTON	1C, 9C
NORTHUMBERLAND PARK	11B	Old Oak Common E Box	1C	PADDOCK WOOD	10D
NORTHWOOD	13B	Old Oak Common W Box	1C	PADGATE	16B
NORTHWOOD HILLS	13B	Old Oak Common W Jnc	9C	Padgate Jnc (Up)	16B
NORTON	7A, 19B	OLD ROAN	23A	Padnall Jnc	11B
NORTON BRIDGE	2A, 8A	Old Shoreham Bridge Box	8D	PAIGNTON	4C
Norton East Jnc	17B	Old Woods Box	10C	Painswick Road (Down)	17A
NORTON FITZWARRREN	2C	OLD WOODS HALT	10C	PAISLEY (CANAL)	31A
NORTON JNC	11C	OLDBURY	5A	PAISLEY (GILMOUR ST)	28A, 31A
Norton South Jnc	17B	OLDFIELD PARK HALT	5C	PAISLEY (ST JAMES)	28A
NORTON-ON-TEES	17B	OLDLAND COMMON	17A	PAISLEY WEST	31A
NORWICH (THORPE)	10B, 12B	Olive Mount Jnc (Up)	9A	PALMERS GREEN	22B
NORWOOD JNC	7D	OLTON	10C	PALNURE	30A
NOSTELL	8B	ONIBURY	2E	PANDY	2E
NOTTINGHAM	14A, 16A	ORBLISTON JNC	34A	PANGBOURNE	5C
NOTTINGHAM (VICTORIA)	14B	Orchardbank (Down)	27A	PANNAL	8B
NOTTINGHAM ROAD	15A	ORDSALL LANE	9A	Pannal Jnc	8B
NUNBURNHOLME	20B	ORE	9D	PANT (SALOP)	13C
NUNEATON (ABBEY ST)	18A	Ore Tunnel	9D	Panteg Jnc	2E
NUNEATON (T.V.)	1A	ORMSIDE	13A	PAR	3C
NUNHEAD	12D	ORMSKIRK	23A	Par Harbour Box	3C
NURSLING	9D	ORPINGTON	10D	PARBOLD	20A
NUTBOURNE HALT	6D	ORRELL	19A	PARK (LMS)	9A
NUTFIELD	13D	ORRELL PARK	23A	PARK (LNER)	28B
Nuttal Tunnel	23A	ORTON	34A	PARK DRAIN	7B
Nutts Lane (Up)	18A	OSMONDTHORPE	8B, 18B	PARKESTON QUAY	12B
O.A.G.B. Jnc (Up)	9A	OSWESTRY	13C	PARKGATE & ALDWARKE	15B
O'MAY	28B	OTFORD	12D	PARKGATE & RAWMARSH	11A
OAKENGATES	10C	Otford A Jnc	12D	PARKHILL	32B
Oakenshaw N Jnc (Down)	11A	OTTERINGTON	3B	Parklee (Up)	28A
Oakenshaw Tunnel	20A	OTTERSPOOL	16B	Parks Bridge Jnc	10D
OAKHAM	14A	Oubeck (Up)	3A	Parkside No 1 (Down)	9A
OAKLE STREET	6C	OUGHTY BRIDGE	14B	Parkside No 2 (Down)	9A
OAKLEIGH PARK	1B	OULTON BROAD SOUTH	12B	PARKSTONE	4D, 1E
Oakleigh Park Tunnel	1B	Ouse Viaduct	7D	PARSON STREET	5C
OAKLEY	10A, 1D	Over Jnc	6C	Parsons Heath Box	9B
Oakley Jnc (Up)	10A	OVERTON	1D	PARTINGTON	16B
Oakley Troughs	10A	OVERTOWN (CLOSED)	27A	Partington Jnc (Up)	16B
OAKSEY HALT	6C	OXENHOLME	3A	PARTON	30A
Oatlands Box	1D	OXFORD	11C	PARTRIDGE GREEN	8D
OBAN	38A	OXFORD (GOODS)	11C	Patcham Tunnel	7D
OCKLEY	6D	Oxford Road Jnc	1C	PATCHWAY & STOKE GIFFORD	7C

PATNEY & CHIRTON	1C	PERSHORE	11C	POKESDOWN	4D
PATRICROFT	9A	PERTH	32A, 24B	POLEGATE	7D, 9D
PAULSGROVE HALT (CLOSED)	5D	PERTH (GENERAL)	26A, 27A	POLESWORTH	2A
Peak Forest	15A	PETERBOROUGH (NORTH)	1B, 5B	Polhill Intermediate Box	10D
Peak Forest Jnc (Down)	15A	PETERHEAD	32B	Polhill Tunnel	10D
PEAKIRK	5B	PETERSFIELD	5D	Pollok Jnc (South)	28A
PEAR TREE & NORMANTON	16A	PETERSTON	7C	Pollok Jnc (Up)	31A
Peascliffe Tunnel	2B	Petteril Bridge Jnc (Down)	14A	POLLOKSHAWS	30A
Peasmarsh Jnc	5D	Petterill Bridge Jnc Box	22B	Polmadie Bridge (Up)	25A
PEBWORTH HALT	12C	Pettimain (Up)	25A	Polmaise (Down)	26A
PECKHAM RYE	6D, 12D	PETTS WOOD	10D	POLMONT	32A, 24B
Peel Hall (Down)	19A	Petts Wood Jnc	10D	Polmont Jnc	32A
PEGSWOOD	3B	PEVENSEY & WESTHAM	9D	Polperro Tunnel	3C
PELAW	17B	PEVENSEY BAY HALT	9D	Polquhap Siding	29A
PEMBERTON	19A, 20A	PEWSEY	1C	PONDERS END	11B
Pemberton Jnc (Up)	19A, 20A	PHILORTH HALT	32B	Ponsandane Siding Box	4C
PEMBREY & BURRY PORT	8C	PHILPSTOUN	32A, 24B	Ponsbourne Tunnel	22B
Penadlake Viaduct	3C	PICCALL	2B	PONT LLIW (GOODS)	8C
PENCOED	7C	PICKHILL	17B	PONTDOLGOCH	13C
PENDAS WAY	8B	PICTON	17B	PONTEFRACT (BAGHILL)	15B
PENDLEBURY	19A	Piershill Jnc Box	4B	PONTHIR	2E
PENDLETON	22A	PILMOOR	3B	PONTRILAS	2E
PENDLETON (BROAD ST)	19A	PILNING	7C	PONTYPOOL ROAD	2E
PENGE EAST	11D	PILSLEY	14B	Pool Hey Jnc (down)	20A
Penge Tunnel	11D	PINCHBECK	6B	POOL QUAY	13C
PENGE WEST	7D	PINHOE	2D	POOLE	4D, 1E
PENISTONE	23A, 14B	PINMORE	31A	Poole Siding	2C
PENKRIDGE	5A	PINNER	13B	Popham Tunnels	4D
Penllergaer Tunnel	8C	PINWHERRY	31A	Port Eglinton Jnc (Overhead)	31A
Penmaenbach Tunnel	6A	Pirbright Jnc	1D	Port Elphinstone	26B
PENMAENMAWR	6A	Pirton Sidings (Down)	17A	PORT GLASGOW	28A
Penmaenmawr Tunnel	6A	PITCAPLE	26B	Port Glasgow Jnc (Up)	28A
PENMAENPOOL	15C	PITLOCHRY	32A	PORT GORDON	27B
Penmaenrhos Tunnel	6A	PITMEDDEN	26B	PORT TALBOT (GENERAL)	7C
PENPERGWM	2E	PITSEA	18A	PORTCHESTER	5D
Penponds Viaduct	3C	PLAISTOW	18A	Portcreek Jnc	5D
PENRHYNDEUDRAETH	15C	PLAWSWORTH	3B	PORTESSIE	27B
PENRITH	3A	PLEAN	26A	PORTKNOCKIE	27B
Penryhn Siding (Down)	6A	PLEASINGTON	23A	PORTLETHEN	27A, 26B
PENSHURST	13D	PLESSEY	3B	PORTMADOC	15C
PENTON	21B	PLOCKTON	37A	PORTOBELLO	4B, 21B
Pentrefelin Siding	15C	PLUCKLEY	10D	Portobello Jnc	21B
Penwithers Jnc	3C	PLUMPTON	3A, 7D	Portobello Jnc (Up)	5A, 7A
PENZANCE	4C	Plumpton (Down)	22A	PORTON	1D
PEPLOW	16C	PLUMSTEAD	8D	Portrack Viaduct	29A
PERRY BARR	7A	PLUMTREE	14A	PORTSKEWETT	6C
Perry Barr N Jnc (Down)	7A	PLYMPTON	3C	PORTSLADE	6D
Perry Barr N Jnc (Up)	5A	POCKLINGTON	20B	PORTSMOUTH & SOUTHSEA (HIGH

LEVEL)	5D	PURTON	6C	RAYNES PARK	1D, 4D
PORTSMOUTH & SOUTHSEA (LOW		PUXTON & WORLE	5C	READING	1C, 5C, 13D
LEVEL)	5D	PWLLHELI	15C	Reading Jnc	13D
PORTSMOUTH ARMS	3D	PYE BRIDGE	11A	Reading W Jnc	5C
PORTSMOUTH CORNHOLME		Pyewipe Jnc	6B, 7B	READING WEST	1C
(CLOSED)	23A	PYLE	7C	Reculver Box	11D
PORTSMOUTH HARBOUR	5D	PYLLE	1E	Red Hill Jnc	2E
PORTSOY	27B	Pylle Hill Jnc	5C	Red Post Jnc	1D
POSSILPARK (GOODS)	28B	QUAINTON ROAD	13B	REDBRIDGE	4D, 9D
POSTLAND	6B	Quainton Road Jnc	13B	Redding	24B
POTTERHANWORTH	6B	Quarry Siding (Down)	20A	REDDISH	8A
POTTERS BAR	1B	QUEEN'S ROAD	1D, 6D	REDHILL	7D, 13D
Potters Bar Tunnel	1B	QUEENS PARK	1A	Redhill Tunnel	7D
Potters Grange Jnc	20B	QUEENSFERRY	6A	Redlake Box	3C
Pottington Box	3D	Queensville (Up)	2A	REDNAL & WEST FELTON	10C
POULTON	21A, 22A	Quintinshill (Up)	24A	REDRUTH (GOODS)	3C
Poulton No 4 (Up)	21A	QUORN	14B	Redruth Jnc	3C
Poulton No 5 (Down)	22A	Race Station	10D	REEDLEY HALLOWS HALT	23A
Pouparts Jnc	7D	RACECOURSE PLATFORM	12C	REIGATE	13D
POWFOOT HALT	29A	RACKS	29A	Relly Mill Jnc	3B
POYNTON	8A	RADCLIFFE BRIDGE	23A	REPTON & WILLINGTON	16A
PREES	7A	Radcliffe N Jnc	23A	RESTON	4B
PRESTATYN	6A	RADFORD	14A	RETFORD	2B, 6B, 16B
Prestatyn Water Troughs	6A	RADIPOLE HALT	4C, 4D	Rhos Jnc	10C
PRESTBURY	8A	RADLETT	10A	RHOSNEIGR	6A
PRESTON	3A, 22A, 23A	RADLEY	11C	RHOSROBIN HALT	10C
PRESTON BROOK	2A	RADSTOCK	1E	RHOSYMEDRE HALT	10C
Preston Hall Tunnels	12D	Rainford Colliery Siding (Up)	19A	RHU	29B
PRESTON JNC	23A	RAINFORD JNC	19A	RHYL	6A
Preston No 5 (Up)	22A	RAINHAM	11D	Rhyl Sands (Up)	6A
PRESTON PARK	7D	RAINHILL	9A	RIBBLEHEAD	12A
PRESTON ROAD	19A	RAMSBOTTOM	23A	RICCARTON JNC	21B
PRESTONPANS	4B	Ramsden Bellhouse Box	12B	RICHBOROUGH CASTLE HALT	11D
PRESTWICK	31A	RAMSGATE	11D	RICKMANSWORTH	13B
PRIESTFIELD	10C	Randolph Siding	25B	RIDDINGS	21B
Primrose Hill Tunnell	1A	Rangeworthy (Up)	17A	RIDDLESDOWN	8D
PRINCES RISBOROUGH	15B, 9C	Rangeworthy Box	12C	Riddlesdown Tunnel	8D
PRINCES ST	27A	RANNOGH	30B	RIDING MILL	22B
PRITTLEWELL	12B	RANSKILL	2B	RIGG	29A
PROBUS & LADOCK PLATFORM	3C	RASKELF	3B	RILLINGTON	19B
Probus Box & Tregagne Viaduct	3C	RATHEN	32B	RIMINGTON	21A
Proof House Jnc	7A	RATHO	32A, 24B	RINGLEY ROAD	23A
Proof House Jnc (Down)	5A, 17A	Rattery Box	3C	RINGWOOD	3D
PRUDHOE FOR OVINGHAM	22B	Ravelrig Jnc (Down)	28A	RIPON	17B
PULBOROUGH	6D	RAVENSBOURNE	12D	Rise Hill Tunnel	13A
PULFORD	10C	RAVENSCRAIG (CLOSED)	28A	RISHTON	23A
PURLEY	7D	RAVENSTHORPE	20A	ROADE	1A, 4A
PURLEY OAKS	7D	RAYLEIGH	12B	ROATH (GOODS)	7C

ROBERTSBRIDGE	13D	Rugby Troughs	1A	Sandling Tunnel	10D
Robin Hood (Up)	22A	RUGELEY	2A	SANDON	8A
Robin Hood Tunnel	23A	RUISLIP & ICKENHAM	15B	Sandridge (Up)	10A
ROBROYSTON	27A	RUISLIP GARDENS	15B, 9C	SANDWICH	11D
ROBY	9A	Rumney Bridge Jnc	7C	SANDY	1B
ROCHDALE	19A	RUNCORN	7A	SANDYCROFT	6A
Rochdale E Jnc (Down)	19A	Runcorn Bridge Viaduct	7A	SANKEY	16B
ROCHESTER	11D	Ruscombe Siding	1C	Sankey Jnc	16B
Rochester Bridge Jnc	8D, 11D	RUSHCLIFFE HALT	14B	Sankey Jnc (Down)	16B
ROCHFORD	12B	Rushey Platt Jnc	5C	SANQUHAR	29A
ROCKCLIFFE	24A	RUSILIP & ICKENHAM	9C	Sapperton Siding	6C
Rockcliffe Hall (Down)	6A	RUSKINGTON	6B	Sapperton Tunnel	6C
ROFFEY ROAD HALT	9D	RUTHERGLEN	25A	SARNAU	8C
ROLLESTON JNC	16A	Rutherglen Jnc (Up)	25A	Saughton Jnc	32A, 24B
ROMFORD	9B	RUTHWELL	29A	SAUNDERTON	15B, 9C
ROMSEY	5D, 9D	RYE	9D	SAVERNAKE	1C
Rookery Bridge (Up)	8A	RYHOPE EAST	17B	SAWBRIDGEWORTH	11B
ROSE GROVE	23A	Ryhope Grange Jnc	17B	SAWLEY (CLOSED)	15A
Rose Grove West (Down)	23A	RYTON	22B	SAWLEY JNC	15A
ROSSETT	10C	S GREENFORD HALT	9C	SAXBY	14A
ROSSINGTON	2B	S HAREFIELD (CLOSED)	15B	Saxelby Tunnel	14A
ROSYTH HALT	24B	S RUISLIP & NORTHOLT JNC	15B, 9C	SAXHAM	7B
ROTHERHAM	14A	SADDLEWORTH	9A	SAXILBY	6B, 7B
ROTHERHAM (MASBOROUGH)	11A	SALFORD	19A	SAXMUNDHAM	10B
ROTHERHAM & MASBORO'	15B	SALFORDS	7D	SCAFELL HALT	13C
ROTHERHAM ROAD	15B	SALHOUSE	10B	SCARBOROUGH	19B, 20B
Rotherwas Jnc	2E	SALISBURY	1D, 5D, 14C	SCAWBY & HIBALDSTOW	23B
ROTHES	27B	SALTAIRE	12A	SCHOLES	8B
ROTHIEMAY	27B	SALTASH	3C	SCOPWICK	6B
ROTHLEY	14B	SALTFORD	5C	SCORRIER	3C
Rothwell Haigh (Up)	11A	SALTLEY	16A, 17A	SCORTON (CLOSED)	3A
Roudham Jnc	11B	SALTMARSHE	20B	SCOTBY	22B
Roundwood (Up)	11A	SALTNEY	10C	SCOTBY (Closed)	14A
ROWLANDS CASTLE	5D	Saltney Holyhead Jnc	10C	SCOTCH DYKE	21B
ROWSLEY	15A	Saltney Jnc (Down)	6A	SCOTSCALDER	36A
ROY BRIDGE	30B	Saltwood Tunnel	10D	SCOTSWOOD	22B
Royal Albert Bridge Box	3C	SALWICK	22A	Scotswood Bridge	22B
Royal Border Bridge	4B	SALZCRAGGIE PLATFORM	36A	Scout Green (Down)	3A
ROYDON	11B	SAMPFORD COURTENAY	2D	Scout Tunnel	9A
ROYSTON	11A, 5B	SAMPFORD PEVERELL	2C	Scratchwood Sidings (Up)	10A
Royston Jnc (Down)	11A, 20A	Sand Street Crossing Box	8D	SCREMERSTON	4B
RUABON	10C, 15C	SANDAL	8B	SCROOBY (CLOSED)	2B
Ruckinge Siding Box	9D	SANDAL & WALTON	11A	Scrooby Water Troughs	2B
RUDDINGTON	14B	SANDBACH	8A	SEABURN	17B
RUFFORD	23A	SANDERSTEAD	8D	SEACROFT	5B
RUGBY	1A, 4A	SANDHILLS	19A, 20A	SEAFORD	7D
RUGBY (CENTRAL)	13B	SANDHURST HALT	13D	SEAHAM	17B
Rugby No 7 (Down)	1A, 4A	SANDLING JNC	10D	SEAMER	19B, 20B

Seamer Jnc	20B	SHEFFIELD	14A	SIDCUP	8D
Sear's Crossing (Down)	1A	SHEFFIELD (VICTORIA)	14B, 15B	SIDLEY	13D
SEATON CAREW	17B	SHELFORD	11B	SIDMOUTH JNC	2D
SEATON JNC	2D	Shelwick Jnc	16C, 2E	Silchester Crossing	4C
Seaton Tunnel	14A	SHENFIELD	9B, 12B	SILEBY	11A
SEEDLEY	9A	SHEPHERDS WELL	12D	Silkstream Jnc (Up)	10A
SEER GREEN	15B	SHEPLEY & SHELLEY	23A	SILVERTON	2C
SEER GREEN HALT	9C	SHEPRETH	5B	Simonswood (Down)	19A
SEFTON PARK	7A	Shepreth Branch Jnc	5B, 11B	SINCLAIRTOWN	25B
SELBY	2B, 18B	SHEPTON MALLET	1E	SINDERBY	17B
SELHURST	7D	SHERBORNE	2D	SINGER	28B
Selkirk Jnc	21B	SHERBURN-IN-ELMET	15B, 19A, 19B	SINGLETON (CLOSED)	22A
SELLING	12D	Sherwood Rise Tunnel	14B	Singleton Bank (Down)	22A
Selling Tunnel	12D	Shieldmuir Jnc (Up)	25A	SITTINGBOURNE	11D
SELLY OAK	17A	SHIELDS ROAD	28A, 31A	SIX MILE BOTTOM	7B
SELSDON	8D	SHIFNAL	10C	SKEGNESS	5B
Selsdon Road Jnc	8D	Shillamill Tunnel	3D	Skelton Jnc	16B
Selside (Down)	12A	Shillingham Tunnel	3C	Skew Crossing (Down)	18A
SEMLEY	2D	SHILLINGSTONE	1E	SKEWEN	8C
SESSAY	3B	SHILTON	1A	Skewen Cutting Box	8C
SETTLE	12A	SHIPLEY GATE	11A	Skewen E Jnc	8C
Settle Jnc (Down)	12A, 18A	SHIPPEA HILL	11B	Skewen W Sidings	8C
SEVEN KINGS	9B	SHIPTON	11C	SKIPTON	12A
SEVENOAKS (TUBS HILL)	10D	SHIREOAKS	16B	Skipton N Jnc (Down)	12A
Sevenoaks Tunnel	10D	Shireoaks East Jnc (Up)	16B	Slade Lane Jnc	8A
Severn Tunnel E Box	7C	SHIRLEY	12C	Slade Lane Jnc (Up)	8A
SEVERN TUNNEL JNC	6C, 7C	Shoe Mill (Up)	23A	Slade Viaduct	3C
Severn Tunnel W Box	7C	SHOEBURYNESS	18A	SLADES GREEN	8D
Sevington Box	10D	SHOLING	9D	Slades Green Jnc	8D
Shaftholme Jnc	19B	SHOREHAM	12D	SLATEFORD	28A
SHAKESPEARE CLIFF HALT	10D	Shoreham Jnc	6D	SLEAFORD	6B
Shakespeare Cliff Tunnel	10D	Shoreham Jnc Box	8D	Sleaford Jnc	5B
SHALFORD	13D	SHOREHAM-BY-SEA	6D	Sleaford N Jnc	6B
Shalford Jnc	5D, 13D	SHORNCLIFFE	10D	Sleaford S Jnc	6B
SHANDON	29B	SHORTLANDS	11D	SLOUGH	1C
SHANKEND	21B	Shortlands Jnc	11D, 12D	SMALL HEATH &	
SHAP	3A	Shortwood Siding (Up)	17A	SPARKBROOK	10C, 12C
Shap Summit (Up)	3A	SHOSCOMBE & SINGLE HILL HALT	1E	Smardale Viaduct	13A
SHAPWICK	1E	Shotlock Hill Tunnel	13A	SMEAFIELD	4B
SHARNBROOK	10A	Shottesbrook Box	1C	Smedley Viaduct (Down)	19A
Sharnbrook Summit	10A	SHOTTON	6A	SMEETH	10D
Shatfholme Jnc	2B	SHOTTS	28A	SMETHWICK	5A
Shawell Box	13B	SHREWSBURY (GENERAL)		SMITHY BRIDGE	19A
SHAWFORD	4D		7A, 10C, 14C, 2E	SNAILHAM HALT	9D
Shawford Jnc	4D	SHRIVENHAM	5C	Snailwell Jnc	7B
SHEEPBRIDGE	14A	Shugborough Tunnel	2A	Snape Jnc	10B
Sheet Crossing Box	5D	SHUSTOKE	18A	Snaygill (Down)	12A
Sheet Stores Jnc (Up)	15A, 16A	SIBSEY	5B	Sneinton Jnc (Up)	16A

SNOWDON HALT	12D	SPEKE (Closed)	7A	St Margarets Tunnel	4B, 21B
Sodbury Tunnel	7C	Speke Jnc (Down)	7A	ST MARY CRAY	11D
SOHAM	7B	Spelbrook	11B	St Mary Cray Jnc	10D, 11D
SOHO	5A	Spetchley (Down)	17A	ST MARY'S CROSSING HALT	6C
SOHO & WINSON GREEN	10C	SPETISBURY HALT	1E	ST MICHAELS	16B
Soho E Jnc (Down)	5A	SPEY BAY	27B	ST NEOTS	1B
SOHO ROAD (Closed)	5A	Spittal Tunnel	8C	ST OLAVES	10B
Soho Soap Works Jnc (Up)	5A	SPOFFORTH	8B	St Olaves Swing Bridge	10B
SOLE ST	11D	SPON LANE	5A	ST PANCRAS	10A
SOLIHULL	10C	SPONDON	15A	St Pinnock Viaduct	3C
Somerhill Tunnel	13D	Spondon Jnc (Up)	15A	ST ROLLOX	27A
SOMERTON	2C	SPOONER ROW	12B	ST THOMAS	2C
Sonning Box	1C	SPRING ROAD	12C	St Vigeans Jnc	26B
Sough Tunnel	21A	SPRING VALE	21A	Stableford (Up)	2A
Souldern Viaduct	9C	SPRINGFIELD	25B	STADDLETHORPE	18B, 20B
Souldrop (Up)	10A	Springs Branch No 1 (Down)	2A	STAFFORD	2A
SOUTH BERMONDSEY	6D	Springwood Jnc (Down)	23A	Stafford Jnc	10C
SOUTH CROYDON	7D	Springwood Tunnel	14B	Stafford No 1	5A
South Croydon Jnc	7D, 8D	SQUIRES GATE	22A	Stafford No 1 (Down)	2A
SOUTH EASTRINGTON	18B	ST ALBAN'S CITY	10A	Stafford Road Jnc	10C
SOUTH ELMSALL	8B	St Andrews Jnc (Up)	16A	STAINFORTH	20B
SOUTH HAMPSTEAD	1A	St Anne's Wood Tunnel	5C	Stainforth Sidings (Up)	12A
SOUTH HAREFIELD (CLOSED)	9C	ST ANNES	22A	STALBRIDGE	1E
SOUTH KENTON	1A	ST AUSTELL	3C	STALLINGBOROUGH	23B
SOUTH MILFORD	18B	ST BOSWELLS	21B	STALYBRIDGE	8A
SOUTH MOLTON ROAD	3D	St Bride's Box	7C	Stalybridge Jnc (Up)	9A
SOUTHALL	1C	St Bride's Crossing	38A	STAMFORD BRIDGE	20B
SOUTHAM ROAD & HARBURY	9C	ST BUDEAUX	3D	Standedge Tunnel	9A
SOUTHAMPTON CENTRAL	4D, 9D	ST BUDEAUX PLATFORM	3C	Standhill Siding	21B
Southborough Viaduct	13D	ST CLEARS	8C	STANDISH	2A
SOUTHBOURNE HALT	6D	ST DENYS	4D, 9D	Standish Jnc	6C, 12C
SOUTHBURN	18B	ST DEVEREUX	2E	Standish Jnc (Up)	17A
Southcote Jnc	1C, 4C	ST DUNSTANS	8B	STANDON BRIDGE	2A
SOUTHEASE HALT	7D	ST ERTH	3C	STANLEY	32A
SOUTHEND EAST	18A	ST FAGANS	7C	STANLEY JNC	26A
SOUTHEND-ON-SEA	18A, 12B	ST FORT	25B	STANNINGLEY	20A, 8B
Southerham Jnc	7D, 9D	ST GERMANS	3C	STANNINGTON	3B
SOUTHPORT (CHAPEL ST)	20A	ST HELENS JNC	9A	STANSFIELD HALL (CLOSED)	
Southport S Jnc (Up)	20A	ST JAMES DEEPING	5B	(TODMORDEN)	23A
SOUTHWAITE	3A	St James Jnc	22B	STANSTED	11B
SOUTHWATER	8D	St James Tunnel	16B	STANTON GATE	11A
SOUTHWICK	30A, 6D	ST JOHN'S	10D	Stanton Tunnel	14A
SOWERBY BRIDGE	19A	St John's Wood Tunnel	13B	STANWARDINE HALT	10C
Sowerby Bridge Tunnel	19A	St Leonard's Bridge (Down)	26A, 27A	Stanway Box	9B
SPALDING	5B, 6B	ST LEONARDS (WARRIOR SQ)	9D	STAPLE HILL FISHPONDS	17A
SPARKFORD	4C	ST LEONARDS (WEST MARINA)	9D	STAPLEFORD	22B
SPEAN BRIDGE	30B	ST LUKE'S	20A	STAPLEFORD & SANDIACRE	11A
SPEETON	20B	St Margarets Jnc	8D	STAPLEHURST	10D

STAPLETON ROAD	12C	STONEHALL & LYDEEN HALT	12D	SUDBURY	15B
Star Lane Box	7D	STONEHAVEN	27A, 26B	SUDBURY HILL	15B
STARCROSS	2C	STONEHOUSE	17A, 6C, 12C	SUMMERSEAT	23A
STAVELEY TOWN	14B	Stonehouse Viaduct	17A, 12C	Summit (Up)	24A
STAVERTON HALT	4C	Stoney Stanton Sidings (Down)	18A	Summit Tunnel E (Down)	19A
Staverton Rd Box	13B	Stoneycombe Siding	2C	Summit Tunnel W (Down)	19A
STECHFORD	5A	Storefield (Down)	14A	SUN BANK HALT	15C
Steel Works (Down)	6A	Stormy Siding	7C	SUNDERLAND	17B
STEELE ROAD	21B	Storrs Mill Jnc (Down)	11A	Sundon (Down)	10A
STEETON	12A	STOULTON	11C	SURBITON	1D
Stenson Jnc (Down)	16A	Stourpaine (Down)	1E	SURFLEET	5B
STEPNEY	18A	STOURPAINE & DURWESTON HALT	1E	SUTTON	6D
STEPPS	27A	Stourton Jnc (Down)	11A	SUTTON BINGHAM	2D
STEVENAGE	1B	STOW	21B	Sutton Branch Jnc	11B
STEVENTON	5C	STOW PARK	7B	Sutton Bridge Jnc	14C
Steventon Box	4D	Stowe Hill Tunnel	1A	Sutton Bridge Jnc (Down)	2E
STEWARTON	29A	STOWMARKET	9B	Sutton Tunnel	7A
STEYNING	8D	Stranraer Harbour Jnc (Up)	31A	SUTTON WEAVER (Closed)	7A
STIRLING	26A	STRANRAER TOWN	31A	SWAINSTHORPE	10B
STOBS	21B	STRAP LANE HALT	2C	SWAN VILLAGE	10C
Stochd Crossing (Up)	33A	STRATFORD	9B	SWANLEY	11D
STOCKINGFORD	18A	STRATFORD-ON-AVON	12C	Swanley Jnc	11D, 12D
Stockingford Tunnel	18A	STRATHBUNGO	30A	SWANSCOMBE HALT	8D
Stockingford Tunnel Sidings (Up)	18A	STRATHCARRON	36A	Swansea Loop West Jnc	8C
STOCKPORT	8A, 16B	STRATHORD	26A	Swansea Valley Jnc	8C
STOCKSFIELD	22B	STRATHORD (CLOSED)	32A	SWANWICK	9D
STOCKSMOOR	23A	STRATHYRE	38A	SWAY	4D
STOCKTON	17B	Strawberry Hill Tunnel	13D	SWAYTHLING	4D
Stodham Crossing Box	5D	Strawfrank Jnc (Down)	25A	Swift's Green Box	10D
STOKE	8A	STREATHAM	6D	SWINDERBY	16A
Stoke Box	1B	STREATHAM COMMON	7D	SWINDON	5C, 6C
STOKE CANON	2C	Streatham Jnc North	7D	Swing Bridge Jnc	32A, 10B, 12B
STOKE EDITH	16C	Streatham Jnc South	6D	Swinlees Jnc (Down)	31A
Stoke Gifford E Box	7C	Streatham Tunnel	6D	SWINTON	11A, 19A, 15B, 22B
Stoke Gifford E Jnc	12C	STRENSALL	19B	Swynnerton Jnc	8A
Stoke Gifford W Box	7C	Stretham Fen Box	11B	SYDENHAM	7D
Stoke Gifford W Jnc	12C	STRETTON	16A	SYDENHAM HILL	11D
Stoke Hammond (Down)	1A	STRICHEN	32B	Sydney Bridge Jnc (Down)	8A
Stoke Jnc (Up)	8A	Stroan Viaduct	30A	Sykes Jnc	6B, 7B
STOKE MANDEVILLE	13B	STROME FERRY	37A	SYSTON	11A
Stoke Tunnel	2B	STROOD	8D	Tackley Box	11C
Stoke Works Jnc (Up)	17A	STROUD	6C	TACKLEY HALT	11C
STONE	8A	STRUAN	32A	TADCASTER	19B
STONE CROSS HALT	9D	Stubbins Jnc (Up)	23A	TAIN	35A
Stone Cross Jnc	7D, 9D	STURMINSTER NEWTON	1E	Tairmeibion (Down)	6A
STONE CROSSING HALT	8D	Sturt Lane Jnc Box	1D	Taitlands Tunnel	12A
STONEA	6B	STURTON	23B	TALACRE	6A
STONEGATE	13D	STYAL	8A	TALERDDIG	13C

TALLINGTON	1B	THORNTON JNC	25B	TORQUAY	4C
TAMERTON FOLIOTT	3D	THORP ARCH	19B	TORRE	4C
TAMWORTH	16A	THORPE BAY	18A	TORRINGTON	2E
TAMWORTII (Low Lcvcl)	2A	THORPE CUIVERT	5B	Torrisholme No 1 (Up)	18A
Tankersley Tunnel	14A	Thorpe Jnc	12B	Torrisholme No 2 (Down)	18A
TAPLOW	1C	THORPE-LE-SOKEN	12B	Torside Crossing	14B
Tapton Jnc (Chesterfield) (Up)	14A	THORPE-ON-THE-HILL	16A	Totley Tunnel	15A
Tapton Jnc (Up)	11A	Thorpes Bridge Jnc (Up)	19A	Totley Tunnel East (Down)	15A
Tarf Viaduct	30A	THREE BRIDGES	7D, 9D	TOTNES	3C
Tattenhall Jnc (Down)	6A	THREE COUNTIES	1B	Toton Centre (Up)	11A
TATTENHALL ROAD	6A	THREE OAKS & GUESTLING HALT	9D	TOTTENHAM (HALE)	11B
TAUNTON	2C	Thrimby Grange (Up)	3A	Tottington Jnc (Up)	23A
TAVISTOCK	3D	Throstle Nest E Jnc (Down)	15A	TOTTON	4D
Tavistock Jnc	3C	Throstle Nest E Jnc (Up)	16B	Touch S Jnc	24B
Tavy Viaduct	3D	Throstle Nest S Jnc (Down)	15A	TOWN GREEN	23A
Tay Viaduct	26A, 27A	THURGARTON	16A	TOWNELEY	23A
TAYNAUILT	38A	Thurgoland Tunnel	14B	Townhill Jnc	24B
TEBAY	3A	Thurmaston (Down)	11A	TRAFFORD PARK	16B
TEIGNMOUTH	2C	THURSO	38A	Trafford Park Jnc (Down)	16B
TEMPLECOMBE	2D, 1E	THURSTON	7B	TRAM INN	2E
TEMPLECOMBE (UPPER) SR	1E	Thurstonland Tunnel	23A	Tramway Jnc	6C
TEMPLEHIRST	2B	Thwaites Jnc (Up)	12A	Treales (Up)	22A
TEMPSFORD	1B	TIBSHELF TOWN	14B	TREETON	11A
TERN HILL	16C	Tiddy Viaduct	3C	Treffgarne Box	8C
TEYNHAM	11D	Tigley Box	3C	Tregeagle Viadcut	3C
Thackley Jnc (Down)	12A	TILE HILL	4A	TREHOWELL HALT	10C
Thackley Tunnel	12A	TILEHURST	5C	TRENT	11A, 16A
THANKERTON	25A	Tilley Crossing	7A	Trent Bridge	6B
THATCHAM	1C	TILLYNAUGHT	27B	Trent Bridge Jncs	7B
THE HAWTHORNS HALT	10C	TINSLEY	15B	Trent Jnc (Down)	11A, 15A
THE LAKES HALT	12C	TIPTON	5A	Trent Viaduct	16A
THE MOUND	35A	TISBURY	1D	TRENTHAM	8A
THE OAKS	21A	Tisbury Gates	1D	Tresulgan Viaduct	3C
THEALE	1C	Tisbury Quarry Crossing Box	1D	Treverrin Box	3C
THETFORD	11B	TIVERTON	2C	Treverrin Tunnel	3C
Thingley Jnc	4C, 5C	TIVETSHALL	10B	Treviddo Viaduct	3C
THIRSK	3B	Toadmoor Tunnel	16A	TREVOR	15C
THORINGTON	12B	TOCHIENEAL	27B	TRING	1A
THORNE	20B	Todderstaffe (Up)	22A	Troon (Old Station) (Up)	31A
Thorne Jnc	20B	TODDINGTON	12C	TROWBRIDGE	4C, 14C
THORNER	8B	TODMORDEN	19A	TROWELL	11A, 14A
THORNHILL	19A, 29A	TOLLERTON	2B	Trowell Moor Sidings	14A
Thornhill L.N.W. Jnc (Down)	19A	TOMATIN	33A	TROWSE (CLOSED)	10B, 12B
Thornhill Midland Jnc	19A	TONBRIDGE	10D, 13D	Trowse Upper Jnc	10B
Thornhill No 1 (Down)	19A	Top of Whiston (Down)	9A	TRURO	3C
Thornhill No 1 (Up)	20A	TORKSEY	6B	Tudeley Box	10D
THORNTON	22A	Torlundy Siding	30B	Tuffley Jnc	6C, 12C
THORNTON HEATH	7D	TORPHINS	28B	Tuffley Jnc (Up)	17A

TULLOGH	30B	Usk Bridge	2E	WARRINGTON (CENTRAL)	16B
TULSE HILL	6D	UTTERBY	5B	WARTHILL	20B
TUNBRIDGE WELLS CENTRAL	13D	VALLEY	7A	Warton (Down)	22A
Tunbridge Wells Goods Box	13D	VAUXHALL	7A, 1D	WARWICK	9C
Tunstead (Up)	15A	VICTORIA	7D, 11D	Waste Bank Tunnel	13A
Turners Lane Jnc (Down)	19A	Victory Siding	2C	WATER ORTON	16A, 18A
TURNHOUSE (CLOSED)	24B	VULCAN HALT	7A	WATERBEACH	11B
TURTON	21A	WADBOROUGH	17A	Waterhouse Siding (Up)	19A
TUTSHILL HALT	6C	WADHURST	13D	WATERLOO	20A, 1D, 10D
TUXFORD (NORTH)	2B	Wadhurst Tunnel	13D	Waterside Jnc	24B
TWEEDMOUTH	4B	WADSLEY BRIDGE	14B	WATFORD JC	1A
Twerton Tunnel	5C	WAINFLEET	5B	Watford Lodge (Down)	4A
Two Mile Bottom Box	11B	WAKEFIELD	19A	Watford S Jnc	13B
TWYFORD	1C	WAKEFIELD (WESTGATE)	8B	Watford Tunnel	1A, 4A
TY CROES	6A	WALCOT	10C	WATH	11A
Tylers Green Box	15B, 9C	WALESWOOD	16B	Wath Rd Jnc (Down)	11A
TYNDRUM	29B	WALKDEN	19A	WATTEN	37A
TYNEHEAD	21B	WALKERINGHAM	7B	WATTON	22B
TYSELEY	10C, 12C	Waller's Ash E Box	4D	WAVERTON	6A
Tyseley S Jnc	10C, 12C	Waller's Ash Tunnel	4D	WAVERTREE	7A
Uddens Crossing Box	3D	WALMER	11D	Wavertree Jnc	7A
UDDINGSTON	25A, 28A	WALSDEN	19A	Weald Intermediate Box	10D
UDNY	32B	WALTHAM	5B	Wearde Box	3C
UFFINGTON	5C	WALTHAM CROSS	11B	Weasal Hall Tunnel	19A
Ulceby Curve Jnc	23B	Waltham Siding	1C	WEASTE (Closed)	9A
ULLESKELF	19B	WALTON JNC	19A, 23A	Weaver Jnc (Down)	2A, 7A
UMBERLEIGH	3D	Walton New Jc (Up)	2A, 7A	WEAVERTHORPE	19B
UNDY HALT	7C	WALTON ON THAMES	1D	Wedgwood Halt	8A
Undy Crossing Box	7C	Walton's Siding (Up)	21A	WEDNESBURY	10C
Unity Brook North (Down)	22A	WAMPHRAY	24A	Wednesfield Heath (Down)	7A
UNSTONE	14A	WANBOROUGH	13D	Wednesfield Heath Tunnel	7A
Uphill Jnc	6C, 14C	Wandelmill (Up)	25A	WEEDON	1A
UPHOLLAND	19A	WANDSWORTH COMMON	7D	WEELEY	12B
UPMINSTER	18A	WANTAGE ROAD	5C	WEETON	8B
UPMINSTER BRIDGE	18A	WARBLINGTON HALT	6D	Weeton (Down)	22A
UPNEY	18A	WARDHOUSE	26B	WELBURY	17B
UPPER BROUGHTON	14A	Wardle (Up)	6A	Welland Viaduct	14A
Upper Denton Box	22B	WAREHAM	4D	Wellhouse Tunnel	23A
UPPER GREENOCK	28A	WARKWORTH	4B	WELLINGBOROUGH	10A
Upper Port Glasgow	30A	Warley (Down)	18A	WELLINGTON	2C, 10C
UPPER WARLINGHAM	8D	WARMINSTER	14C	WELLOW	1E
UPTON MAGNA	10C	WARMLEY	17A	Wells Tunnel	13D
UPTON PARK	18A	WARMSWORTH (CLOSED)	22B	WELSH HOOK HALT	8C
UPWEY JNC	4C, 4D	WARNHAM	6D	WELSHAMPTON	13C
UPWEY WISHING WELL HALT	4C, 4D	WARREN HALT	10D	WELSHPOOL	13C
URMSTON	16B	Warren Hill Jnc	7B	WELTON	1A
URQUHART	27B	WARRINGTON	7A	WELWYN GARDEN CITY	1B
Usan Box	26B	WARRINGTON (BANK QUAY)	2A	WELWYN NORTH	1B

Welwyn North Tunnel	1B	WESTHOUSES & BLACKWELL	11A	WHITTINGTON (LOW LEVEL)	10C
Welwyn South Tunnel	1B	WESTON	8A, 17A	WHITTLESFORD	11B
Welwyn Viaduct	1B	WESTON-RHYN	10C	Whitwood (Up)	19A
WEM	7A	WESTON-SUB-EDGE	12C	Wichnor Jnc (Down)	16A
WEMBLEY FOR SUDBURY	1A	WESTON-SUPER-MARE	14C	WICK	37A
WEMBLEY HILL	15B	Westonmill Viaduct	3C	WICKFORD	12B
WEMYSS BAY	28A	Westward Park (Down)	19A	WICKHAM MARKET	10B
Wemyss Bay Jnc (Down)	28A	Westwood Viaduct	3C	WICKWAR	17A, 12C
WENDOVER	13B	WETHERAL	22B	Wickwar Tunnel	17A, 12C
WENNINGTON	18A	WETHERBY	8B	WIDDRINGTON	3B
Wensum Jnc	10B	Wetherby E Jnc	19B	Widehough Box	22B
WENTWORTH	14A	Wetherby W Jnc	8B, 19B	WIDMERPOOL	14A
Werrington Jnc	5B	Wetmore Siding (Up)	16A	Widnes East Jnc (Down)	16B
Werrington Jnc Box	1B	WEYBRIDGE	1D	WIDNEY MANOR	10C
Werrington Water Troughs	1B	WEYMOUTH	4C, 4D	WIGAN (N.W.)	2A
WEST ALLERTON	7A	Weymouth Jnc	4C, 4D	WIGAN (WALLGATE)	20A
WEST BROMWICH	10C	WHALLEY	21A	WIGSTON (GLEN-PARVA)	18A
WEST DRAYTON & YIEWSLEY	1C	Wharncliffe Branch Jnc (Up)	14A	WIGSTON (MAGNA)	10A
WEST DULWICH	11D	WHATSTANDWELL	15A	Wigston N Jnc (Down)	18A
WEST EALING	1C, 9C	Wheal Busy Siding	3C	Wigston N Jnc (Up)	10A
WEST FERRY	25B	Wheatsheaf Jnc	10C	WILBRAHAM ROAD	16B
WEST GRINSTEAD	8D	Wheldale Colliery	19A	WILLASTON	7A, 16C
WEST HAM	18A	WHETSTONE	13B	WILLENHALL	7A
WEST HAMPSTEAD	10A	WHIFFLET (LOW LEVEL)	26A	WILLERSEY HALT	12C
WEST HARTLEPOOL	17B	WHIMPLE	2D	Willersley Tunnel	15A
WEST HOATHLEY	8D	Whisker Hill Jnc (Down)	16B	WILLESDEN JC	1A
West Largin Viaduct	3C	WHISSENDINE	14A	Willingdon Jnc	7D
West London Jnc	1D	WHISTLEFIELD	29B	WILLOUGHBY	5B
WEST MOORS	3D	WHITACRE	18A	WILMCOTE	12C
WEST PENNARD	1E	WHITCHURCH	7A, 13C, 1D	WILMSLOW	8A
WEST ST LEONARDS	13D	White Horse Farm Tunnel	15B, 9C	WILNECOTE	16A
WEST TIMPERLEY	16B	Whiteball Siding	2C	WILPSHIRE	21A
WEST WEYBRIDGE	1D	Whiteball Tunnel	2C	Wilsontown S Jnc (Down)	28A
WEST WORTHING	6D	Whitehall Jnc (Down)	11A	WILTON	14C, 1D
WEST WYCOMBE	15B	Whitehouse S Jnc (Up)	23A	WIMBLEDON	1D
West Wylam Box	22B	WHITEHURST HALT	10C	WINCANTON	1E
WESTBOURNE PARK	1C, 9C	Whitemoor Jnc	6B	WINCHBURGH (CLOSED)	32A
WESTBURY	1C, 4C, 14C	Whitemoss (Up)	26A	Winchburgh Jnc	24B, 32A
WESTBURY-ON-SEVERN HALT	6C	WHITLAND	8C	WINCHCOMBE	12C
WESTCALDER	28A	WHITLINGHAM	10B	WINCHELSEA	9D
WESTCLIFF-ON-SEA	18A	WHITLOCKS END HALT	12C	WINCHESTER	4D
WESTCOMBE PARK	8D	WHITMORE	2A	Winchester Jnc	4D
WESTENHANGER	10D	Whitmore Troughs	2A	WINCHFIELD	1D
WESTERFIELD	10B	Whitrope Box	21B	WINCHMORE HILL	22B
Westerleigh N Jnc	17A, 12C	Whitrope Tunnel	21B	WINCOBANK	14A
Westerleigh W Jnc	7C, 12C	WHITSTABLE & TANKERTON	11D	Wincobank Stn Jnc (Chaletown Loop	
WESTERTON	28B	WHITTINGTON	11A	[Up])	14A
WESTGATE-ON-SEA	11D	WHITTINGTON (HIGH LEVEL)	13C	Windmill Bridge Jnc	7D

Windsor Bridge No 1 (Up)	19A	
Windsor Bridge No 3 Jnc (Up)	19A, 22A	
Wing Sidings (Down)	14A	
Wing Tunnel	14A	
WINGFIELD	16A	
Wingfield Tunnel	16A	
WINNERSH HALT	13D	
WINSFORD	2A	
Winsford Jc (Up)	2A	
WINSON GREEN	5A	
Winsor Hill	1E	
Winsor Hill Tunnel	1E	
Winstanley Colliery Siding (Up)	19A	
WINTERBOURNE	7C, 12C	
Winterbutlee Tunnel	19A	
Winwick Jnc (Up)	2A, 7A	
Winwick Quay (Up)	2A, 7A	
Winwick Road (Up)	16B	
WISHAW CENTRAL	27A	
Wishaw N Jnc	27A	
WISHAW SOUTH	25A	
WISHFORD	14C	
Wiske Moor Water Troughs	3B	
WISTANSTOW HALT	2E	
Wistow (Up)	10A	
WITHAM	9B, 2C	
WITHINGTON	15A, 16C	
WITLEY	5D	
WITTON	7A	
WIVELSFIELD	7D	
WIVENHOE	12B	
WOKING	1D, 5D	
Woking Jnc	1D, 5D	
WOKINGHAM	13D	
WOLDINGHAM	8D	
Wolfhall Jnc	1C	
WOLFS CASTLE HALT	8C	
Wollaton Colliery Sidings (Up)	14A	
Wolvercot Jnc	11C	
WOLVERCOT PLATFORM (CLOSED)	11C	
WOLVERHAMPTON	5A, 10C	
WOLVERTON	1A	
WOMBWELL	14A	
WOMERSLEY	19B	
WOOD END	12C	
WOOD GREEN	7A, 1B	
Wood Green Tunnel	1B	
WOODBOROUGH	1C	
WOODBRIDGE	10B	
Woodburn Jnc	14B, 15B	
Woodfidley Gates	4D	
WOODFORD	13B	
WOODHEAD	14B	
Woodhead Tunnel	14B	
WOODHOUSE	14B	
Woodhouse E Jnc	14B, 16B	
WOODHOUSE MILL	11A	
Woodlands Box	2C	
WOODLESFORD	11A	
WOODLEY	16B	
Woodmuir Jnc (Down)	28A	
Woodsford Crossing Box	4D	
WOODSIDE	26B, 32B	
Woodside Sdg (Up)	7A	
WOOFFERTON	2E	
WOOL	4D	
WOOLASTON	6C	
Woolmer Green Box	1B	
WOOLSTON	9D	
WOOLWICH ARSENAL	8D	
WOOLWICH DOCKYARD	8D	
WOOTTON BASSETT	5C, 7C	
Wootton Bassett Incline Box	5C	
Wootton Box	4D	
WOOTTON RIVERS	1C	
WOOTTON WAWEN PLATFORM	12C	
WORCESTER (SHRUB HILL)	11C, 16C	
WORCESTER PARK	4D	
Worgret Jnc	4D	
WORKSOP	16B	
Worle Jnc	5C, 14C	
WORLESTON	6A	
WORMALD GREEN	17B	
WORPLESDON	5D	
WORSTEAD	10B	
WORTHING CENTRAL	6D	
Worting Jnc	1D, 4D	
WORTLEY	14B	
Wortley Jnc (Down)	11A	
WOTTON	15B	
WRABNESS	12B	
WRAFTON	3D	
WRANGATON	3C	
Wrawton Jnc	23B	
WREA GREEN	22A	
WREAY (CLOSED)	3A	
WRENBURY	7A	
Wrenthorpe N Jnc	8B	
WRESSLE	18B	
WREXHAM	10C	
Wrexham Colliery Siding	10C	
Wright's Siding	15C	
Wrine Hill (Down)	2A	
WROXHAM	10B, 12D	
Wye Valley Jnc	6C	
WYKE	20A	
Wyke Crossing Box	2D	
Wyke Jnc (Up)	20A, 23A	
Wyke Tunnel	20A	
WYLAM	22B	
WYLIE	14C	
WYMONDHAM	12B	
Wymondham Jnc (Up)	14A	
WYNNVILLE HALT	10C	
WYRE DOCK	22A	
WYRE HALT	11C	
YARDLEY WOOD	12C	
YARM	17B	
YARMOUTH (SOUTH TOWN)	10B	
YARNTON	11C	
YATE	17A, 12C	
Yate S Jnc	17A, 12C	
YATTON	5C	
YAXLEY	1B	
YEOFORD	2D	
YEOVIL (PEN MILL)	4C	
YEOVIL JNC	2D	
YETMINSTER	4C	
YNYSLAS	13C	
YOCKLETON	14C	
YORK	2B, 19B, 20B	
YORTON	7A	

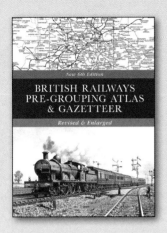
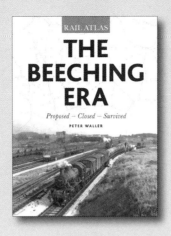
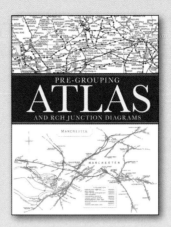
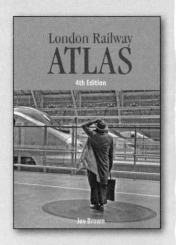

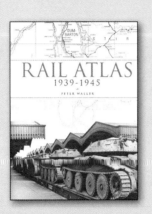
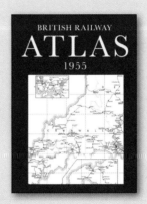
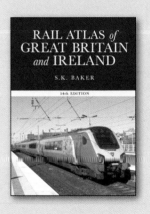
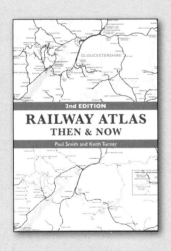
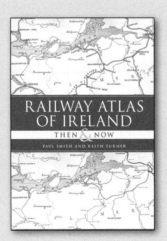
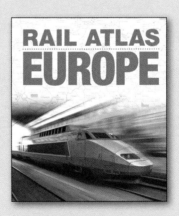